MW00955626

Be an Explorer. Not a Tourist.

…and Travel With Integrity.

It feels good to support the people and places in this book.

We are about to introduce you to good people,

good places and good businesses that deserve your time.

ALEXA WEST GUIDES

Mexico City, 2023

Copyright © 2023 The Solo Girl's Travel Guide™

All rights reserved. No part of this publication may be reproduced or copied or transmitted in any form, physical or electronic, or recorded without prior permission from The Solo Girl's Travel Guide™

Please contact us at hello@thesologirlstravelguide.com

The Solo Girl's Travel Guide updates this book series year-round, as businesses grow, change, and even sometimes, close. A quick double-check before you drive an hour to a restaurant is always a safe practice - as these things are out of our control. And hey, if you see a change we should know about – we'd love it if you let us know so we can update our guide for future travelers.

STOCK OUR BOOK

Want to stock our book in your shop, store, or platform? Send us a message at hello@thesologirlstravelguide.com

Cover & Book Design by Emilia Igartua Vellatti

@__helloemilia

MEXICO CITY

ALEXA WEST GUIDES

EVERY GIRL SHOULD TRAVEL SOLO
AT LEAST ONCE IN HER LIFE

You don't need a boyfriend, a travel partner or anyone's
approval to travel the world. And you don't need a massive
bank account or an entire summer off work.

All you need is that wanderlust in your blood and a good
guidebook in your hands.

If you've doubted yourself for one moment, remember this:

Millions of girls travel across the globe all by themselves every
damn day and you can, too.

You are just as capable, just as smart, and just as brave as the
rest of us. You don't need permission – this is your life.

Listen to your gut, follow your heart and remember that the
best adventures start with the simple decision to go.

Nice to meet you!
I'm Lexi...

I'm not here to get rich or reach 1 million followers on Instagram. I'm here because I want to change the way we travel as women.

I want to help you find yourself.

I want to fling you to the other side of the world, out of your comfort zone (but still safe, I got you), and help you get so totally lost that you find yourself.

And I do that by connecting you to the most beautiful places, the kindest people, the most challenging opportunities, and the most rewarding experiences.

Do you know what kind of woman this will create?

A happy woman who shines so bright that everyone she comes in contact with is illuminated too.

I'm here to turn your light up, girl.

I'm here to help you connect to the experiences that will change you. ...and get the best Instagram photos, too, of course.

To glow up on your travels, remember Travel Karma is real and beautiful.

Travel to give and you will get.

A LITTLE ABOUT ME

Back in 2010, I was a broke-ass Seattle girl who had just graduated from college and had about $200 to my name. I was faced with two choices: get a job, a husband, and have 3 babies plus a mortgage...or sell everything I owned, travel the world and disappoint my parents.

Obviously, I made the right choice.

For the past 10 years, I've been traveling the world solo. I've played every travel role from being the young volunteer and broke backpacker to flying to exotic islands to review new luxury hotels and give breath to struggling tourism industries.

Now I spend my days as an explorer on a mission to change the way that women travel the world. I want to show you places you've never seen and unlock hidden doors you never knew existed in places you may have been before. I want to create a path for you where you feel safe while diving deeper into cultures and countries beyond your own – whether for a week, a year, or a lifetime. And that's what I'm doing.

xoxo, Alexa West

FIND MY MEXICO CITY PLAYLIST HERE

Flights, airports, walking around town...

Travel is a little bit more magical when good music is involved.

ALEXA'S #1 TIP FOR MAKING FRIENDS AS A SOLO TRAVELER:

Put your damn phone down.

You didn't come all the way here just to scroll on Instagram, now did you?

People are less likely to approach you when you look so busy on your phone. You have no shot of making eye contact with a stranger if you're staring at reading internet gossip. You miss every opportunity that you do not see.

The next time you're sitting at a bar or on the beach and you have nothing to entertain you, resist the urge to pick up your phone. Resist the addiction. Instead, journal while taking time to look around. Listen to music with one headphone in. Or just sit and watch people walking by.

Hell, next time you need directions, put the phone down. Ask a human. Give yourself every chance to make human contact and watch your world spin into beautiful circumstances you never could have planned.

Want more travel tips?
Join Alexa's travel tip email series. This will change how you travel forever.

Go to Alexa-West.com and sign-up for her newsletter.

Hello, I'm Emilia...

Have you ever felt stuck and stagnant, like there's got to be more to life? It was 2019 and I was feeling juuuust like that. So I decided to travel far away from my routine, alone. I bought a ticket to Bali, along with a certain travel guide that changed my life: The Solo Girl's Travel Guide to Bali.

I spent 1.5 months exploring the island, following my travel guide, visiting temples, exploring the depths of the ocean, and making new friends...but most of all, getting to know myself. My solo trip was an IV drip for my very dehydrated soul. It brought me back to life and unlocked a whole new world of possibilities I never knew existed. The trip was a success.

And just when my 1-month exploration was ending, when I was supposed to return home...the pandemic happened. I got stuck in Bali indefinitely and thank goodness I did, because serendipity brought me to Alexa. She quickly became my soul sister and partner in crime, and now we are changing the way and why women travel.

These days, Alexa and I spend our days creating books and spaces for badass girls who want to step out of their comfort zones and live a life of wander and wonder.

Oh and did I mention that I'm Mexican? Like, born and raised in Mexico.

I know, I know, my English is amazing – I get that a lot. So just know that The Solo Girl's Travel Guide's Mexico series is filled with my local girl knowledge, tips, friends, beaches and adventures that no gringo would ever know about…

So follow this guide, and follow your gut. You'll find nothing but magic ahead.

Con amor, Emilia

AN IMPORTANT NOTE FOR NOMADS...

Mexico City is becoming a digital nomad hub. More and more travelers are flocking to this incredible hotspot to stay, work, and explore for months at a time.

But there's an issue which comes along with this wave of digital nomads: gentrification.

The city is becoming more expensive, nice apartments are becoming Airbnbs and more chains are moving into the city.

How can you help?

→ Buy your groceries in local "tienditas" (grocery stores) instead of big supermarkets

→ Frequent local coffee shops instead of Starbucks - the same goes for all chains vs. local establishments.

→ Make an effort to learn Spanish.

→ When possible, stay in hotels or guest houses rather than Airbnbs.

You can't stop Mexico City from attracting travelers who want to stay - but you can do your part to travel here more responsibly and make an effort not to contribute to this gentrification.

-EMILIA

TABLE OF CONTENTS

SEE A GIRL TRAVELING WITH THIS GEAR?

SAY HI.

SHE'S YOUR SISTER IN THE

Solo Girl's Travel Club

CARRY THIS GEAR AS AN INVITATION TO FRIENDSHIP

GET IT HERE

OR AT ALEXA-WEST.COM

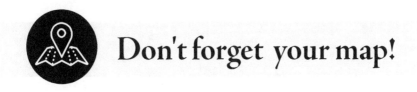

Don't forget your map!

You will find maps in this book - but general maps to give you general ideas. For detailed maps on your phone that will ACTUALLY help you find the things in this book, follow these steps:

1. Scan the QR Code.

SCAN ME!

2. Once the map opens up in your Google Maps, it's automatically saved in your account!

3. Browse. Get a mental idea of where is what.

4. To find your map just tap on Saved on the bottom bar, and then on Maps, on the bottom right of your screen.

Now you're prepared.

....

Bonus! Download GoogleMaps Offline like this...

Step 1: Open GoogleMaps

Step 2: In the search bar, type "Okay Maps".

Step 3. Select the vicinity to download (usually a city or neighborhood) and click download.

....

Want more travel tips?

Join Alexa's travel tip email series. This will change how you travel forever.

Go to Alexa-West.com and sign-up for her newsletter.

Mexico City

MEXICO CITY

INTRODUCTION TO MEXICO CITY

Welcome to the biggest city in North America.

Often described as the "New York City of Latin America", Mexico City, like NYC, is composed of boroughs or delegaciones. Each delegation is divided by "colonias" or neighborhoods. And each neighborhood offers its own vortex of culture, history and food. You could literally hop from one neighborhood to another and experience a totally different version of the city (and a totally different version of you).

On the other hand, some people describe Mexico City as feeling like a little piece of Europe thanks to the incredible architecture, history, museums, castles and fashion. As you'll soon discover, there is so much more to Mexico City than tacos (although, you're going to be obsessed with the tacos)!

A little background: Mexico City has actually been a mecca for commerce since pre-Hispanic times. Tenochtitlan, Mexico City's original name, was the greatest city in Mesoamerica and the reigning capital of the Aztec Empire until 1521, when both the empire and the city were "conquered" by the Spanish (hence, how Mexico adopted the Spanish language and Catholicism). While Spanish culture permeated the population, Mexico City never truly lost its essence. Instead, it became a melting pot where indigenous and Hispanic cultures merged together.

Through the years, Mexico City has stood tall through the Spanish conquest, wars, revolutions, floods, and earthquakes. It's resilient. Like trees or mountains, Mexico City's history can be read through its layers of architecture.

This is a city that you'll never finish getting to know so no matter how many times you visit and re-visit, so where do you even begin?

First, let us remind you that this guide was written by a Mexican girl whose family has long roots in Mexico City, and by her gringa partner who got lost, confused, and curious enough to ask the right questions. Together, we've created a comprehensive yet absorbable guide for you to dive deep beneath the touristy surface to truly explore Mexico City like a local.

This book is your ticket to navigating this city easily and effortlessly, discovering new slices of culture, spirituality and food each time you visit.

Let's start with the basics, shall we?

The Quick Facts

Language: Spanish

Population: Over 21 million

Total Area: 573 square miles

Currency: Mexican Peso

Time Zone: Central Daylight Time (GMT -5)

Religion: Roman Catholic

PRO TIP! See "CDMX" everywhere? That's short for "Ciudad de Mexico", the official name in Spanish of Mexico City.

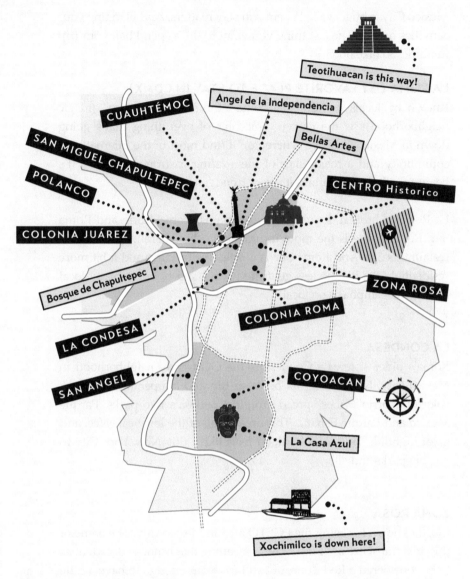

Teotihuacan is this way!

Angel de la Independencia

Bellas Artes

CUAUHTÉMOC

SAN MIGUEL CHAPULTEPEC

CENTRO Historico

POLANCO

COLONIA JUÁREZ

Bosque de Chapultepec

ZONA ROSA

COLONIA ROMA

LA CONDESA

SAN ANGEL

COYOACAN

La Casa Azul

Xochimilco is down here!

Areas to Know
in Mexico City

___

⬚ FREEWAYS ⌐ ¬ AVENUES ||||| AIRPORT

Mexico City is huge, ya'll. Where you stay matters. And planning your activities matter. The last thing you want to do is spend half your trip in traffic. So take note!

LA ROMA (MY FAVORITE PLACE TO STAY IN CDMX)

Known by locals as "Colonia Roma", this "barrio magico" (magic neighborhood) is the current epicenter of everything that's going down in Mexico City. It's where you'll find most of the international community and a major slice of the sizzling gastronomic scene. It's beautiful, it's walkable, and it's very trendy.

La Roma is broken down into two sections: Roma Norte and Roma Sur. Roma Norte is the more fashionable side, where most bars and restaurants are. And Roma Sur is a little less buzzing and a bit more residential (aka it's the less gentrified part), and home to many local food gems - emphasis on local.

LA CONDESA

Roma's older sister. La Condesa is the OG trendy neighborhood in Mexico City. Now it's a mix between hip and happening and local, colorful "barrio" vibes spread around Condesa's two parks: Parque Mexico and Parque España. This area is full of the loveliest cafes, and great nightlife. This neighborhood feels like a tiny New York City to me, big parks and all.

ZONA ROSA

Mostly known for being the LGBTQ area in Mexico City. The name of this area translates as "Pink Zone"...meaning that is not as decadent as to be considered a Red Zone, but still frivolous enough to have a little color on its cheeks. This neighborhood is full of random little treasures. From Korean karaokes at night, to world-class bakeries during the day.

I often stay in Zona Rosa if I can find an amazing hotel deal that is cheaper than La Roma Norte, but still within walking distance to La Roma Norte.

LA JUAREZ

Colonia Juarez has officially become an extension of La Roma. Hip bars and restaurants in a local, classical neighborhood. It's where you'll find the most happening nightlife, so it's sort of La Roma's playground when the lights go down.

CUAUHTEMOC

And just North of Colonia Juarez, you'll find Colonia Cuahutemoc, a tiny neighborhood that's also a star on the rise as chefs and restaurateurs are starting to migrate north from La Roma and La Juarez to this area. But beyond the trendy spots, this area is a true glimpse into local city life. Cuauhtemoc is a business hub, surrounded by skyscrapers packed with offices. Walk around at lunch and you'll see everyone rushing to and from their lunch break.

Ps. Cuauhtemoc. pronounced "kwau-te-mok".

SAN MIGUEL CHAPULTEPEC

A small, subtly elegant neighborhood that stands between Condesa and Chapultepec. This area is so tiny and residential that it's often overlooked by travelers, but its beloved by residents in-the-know because the place to go for an art safari (aka gallery hopping). But also because this neighborhood is your gateway to Bosque de Chapultepec, Mexico City's Central Park, and everything you can see and do within it.

CENTRO HISTORICO

The first time I came to Centro Historico, I felt like I was in Europe from the marvelous historic building and architecturally wondrous plaza... with a McDondalds on the ground floor. It's absolutely breathtaking and convenient. Centro Historico is the perfect representation of the area: old mixed with new. In the Historic District of Mexico City, life circles around The Zocalo, the largest plaza in Latin America which holds nearly 100,000 people. This plaza is lined with the most stunning buildings that light up at night (you must try to come and see this!).

Come to eat or drink at some of the most trendy rooftop bars with stunning views of the city. You'll find a few good hostels in this area, too!

POLANCO

Welcome to one of the bougiest corners of Mexico. This posh upper-class neighborhood is all about shopping, dining and drinking...and yes, you will need a reservation well in advance if you want to get into some of Polanco's hotspots. This mecca for socialites is home to some of the best restaurants and bars in Latin America, as well as some theaters, museums and cultural corners. It's also home to Mexico's own "Fifth Avenue", an avenue lined up with high end stores and marble sidewalks. (Yes, actual marble.)

Ps. People watching here is freaking fantastic. The Botox has gone wild in Polanco!

COYOACAN & SAN ANGEL

A small town trapped in a city! Coyoacan is famous for being the home and birthplace of iconic painter Frida Kahlo and of La Casa Azul, Frida's former house that is now a museum. This area is all about art and history...plus a really great traditional market with incredible food. But it's also becoming a happening neighborhood full of quirky cafes sprinkled along its cobbled stone streets.

Right below Coyoacan is San Angel, another little small Mexican postcard of a town engulfed by the concrete jungle. San Angel would seem like a prime tourist spot, but it's actually usually overlooked by visitors. It's the place to go for a dip in Mexican culture in their traditional Saturday indoor market, El Bazar del Sabado. Consider staying here to get off the beaten path.

OTHER AREAS TO KNOW ABOUT...

SANTA FE
The metropolis of the metropolis. Far away from the historical areas and barrio life, Santa Fe is one of CDMX's newest neighborhoods and the business center of the city. This area is not worth visiting if you're just traveling (it can feel like going to work with your dad) but if you decide to stay longer, there's a good bar and restaurant scene to check out.

AVENIDA PASEO DE LA REFORMA
Ok, so this isn't a neighborhood, but this avenue is one of the city's main veins. It runs diagonally through the CDMX and was built in the 1860s modeled after the big European avenues of the time. Nowadays it's home to many of the tallest buildings, and of course, to the iconic Angel de la Independencia monument.

WHAT ARE THESE? Jacaranda Trees
If you come to Mexico City in the Spring… you'll see these beautiful blooming purple trees everywhere. They were first brought to Mexico from Brazil by a Japanese immigrant and flower expert, Tatsugoro Matsumoro. He was commissioned by president Alvaro Obregon to plant these trees to beautify the city right after the Revolutionary War. And since then, every spring we can enjoy the city painted in purple with these flowers. The original trees first planted by Matsumoro still stand along Paseo de la Reforma.

PRO TIP! Come in spring to see the purple Jacaranda trees lining the avenue in full bloom. The whole city is covered in purple during this season.

Mexico City 101

THE FOOD

Most of your days in CDMX will revolve around food. Bring your stretchy pants.

Yes, of course your mind will be blown by the local food in Mexico City. Tacos, tortas, tlayudas, chilaquiles, moles, tlacoyos and more things you've never heard of! There is a whole universe of Mexican food waiting to be explored on the streets, in the markets and in little bistros. This is a city that requires a local street food tour!

But beyond traditional delights, you'll find some of the greatest chefs in the world who have turned Mexico City into one of the most epic food scenes on the planet. From authentic Singaporean chicken and sushi that will blow your mind to 8-course small plate set menus that require reservations made months in advance...I'm telling you, you've never experienced food like this! Mexico City has it all...but at half the price that you're probably used to.

Ps. Mexican food is all about the meat! But if you're vegan or vegetarian, don't worry. You'll find all sorts of inclusive foodie options in this modern city.

THE RELIGION

Time for a quick history lesson. Mexico, prior to the European arrival, was populated by advanced ancient civilizations such as the Mayans and the Aztecs (think pyramids and hieroglyphics). These civilizations developed complex cultures, systems and even polytheist religions where they worshiped deities related to nature and other intangible concepts such as destiny and fortune.

But then the Spanish came and ruined all that cool stuff. The Spanish conquered the area, building churches on top of pyramids and temples, and replacing the many ancient gods with Jesus Christ and the Holy Trinity. Today, Mexico as we know it is a Roman Catholic country rather than the mystical one it could have been.

However, there has been a slow revival of the spiritual world. These ancient beliefs and traditions have been making a comeback, evolving and swirling around with the modern-day world. In Mexico, you'll find the most devoted Catholics. But you will also find empty churches in southern rural towns where natives sacrifice chickens following pre-Hispanic rituals.

In this book, I cannot wait to give you the keys to unlock your own spiritual path in Mexico. No chicken sacrifices required, I promise.

THE PEOPLE

Mexico City is BIG. Big as in New-York-kinda big, but even more so. Here, you have people from every walk of life from Mexico and beyond. You can find generations of locals who have literally been raised in the market stalls. They were born and raised knowing nothing but the markets. In these market cultures, Mexican urban folklore is what they eat, sleep and breathe! More on this later.

But you can also find Mexicans who speak English with an undetectable accent because they're posh and well traveled. You have the entire spectrum of society represented in this metropolis. Beyond that, Mexico City has become a city not only for native Mexicans, but also a home for big Argentinean, French, American and Spanish communities, among so many other nationalities. The expat population is growing by the day. To sum it up, it's hard to pinpoint the exact avatar of the people in Mexico City because there is not one specific type.

In general, however, Mexicans here are friendly, smiley and warm people that won't hesitate to give you directions or recommendations whenever you need them. That being said, there are some neighborhoods and markets which you should not go alone. Let's talk about it real quick.

THE CRIME

When you told people you were going to Mexico City, they probably freaked out, right? They imagine that you'll be mugged and kidnapped and you'll be miserable and die! Umm, not really. True, Mexico, and specifically Mexico City, has a gritty reputation. Mostly dragged from a darker period back in the 90s. But the city has become safer and safer in the past 10 years…parts of it at least.

If you look up Mexico City's crime index, it reports a "high" rating. But that's just because there's a bunch of bad eggs in some bad neighborhoods. And guess what? You're not going to any of those sketchy areas of town (except for this one taco spot…but I'll walk you through that later). This book is going to steer you clear of the sketchy spots and guide you towards the safest neighborhoods.

And of course, follow your common sense and basic safety guidelines. I'm also going to give you a full safety checklist in my Safe Girl Tips section on page 76. Follow this book and that chapter, and you'll be just as safe here as in NYC. If your mom is still nervous about you going, just have her message me.

THE EARTHQUAKES

Remember those earthquake drills you used to do in school? Most likely you never needed to use them, but it's good to know what to do just in case. So! I'd rather you know about the earthquakes in Mexico City than be happily oblivious and surprised if you feel one. The fact is that Mexico City sits in a seismic zone called "Ring of Fire" which runs along the Pacific Ocean. It's where 90 percent of the world's seismic activity happens. Mexico trembles almost every day. But when there's major seismic activity, it's mostly felt in the southern parts of Mexico.

Most of the time, these earthquakes go unnoticed. In fact, Emy has been in Mexico City when earthquakes have been reported and she barely felt a thing! But on a few occasions, bigger earthquakes have hit the city and it's important to be prepared just in case.

NOT-SO-FUN MEXICO CITY FACT:

The latest big earthquake happened on September 19th, 2017. The city was hit with a 7.1 earthquake and shook for about 20 seconds. Strangely, the date coincided with the 32nd anniversary of a devastating earthquake that happened in 1985. Every September 19th you'll see memorials and mandatory drills all across town.

THE VOLTAGE

Mexico's voltage is 127 Volts / 60 Hz frequency, same as in the USA and Canada. So don't worry, you won't need to be hauling around any chunky adapters! However, depending on where you're staying, you might find Type A plugs (you know, those that only have the two flat thingys). So, if your charger / cord is Type B (two flat contact pins plus a third cylindrical one...) make sure to bring those ones so you can plug in anywhere.

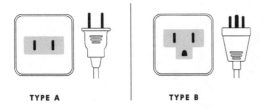

TYPE A   **TYPE B**

Unless you're carrying sensitive electronics (like said hair dryer) you won't need an international adapter which converts the actual voltage.

You'll just need a plug adapter, like this ☞

#ASKTHEMEXICAN

Do you have any specific questions about Mexico?
As your designated local guide, I'm always happy to respond to any doubts about my country.

Shoot me your questions via DM at @__helloemilia or email me at emilia@thesologirlstravelguide.com

Bring This Book to Life –

CHECK OUT OUR MEXICO CITY HIGHLIGHTS ON INSTAGRAM

SEE YOU THERE!

WANT THIS BOOK IN FULL COLOR?

Did you know everything
Solo Girl's Travel Guide is made
by just two girls?

That's right, we're Indie Authors...
And if we print color, it's oh-so expensive.

But if you'd like a beautiful color digital copy, get the
digital version on Etsy.

Psst. If you have the paperback book, you can get the
digital copy for a VIP price. Use code <u>VIPReader</u>

MEXICO CITY

Survival Guide

●─────────────────●

●─────────────────●

The Weather

When to Visit:

If you have vacation time to use, use it! Any time of year is good to travel to Mexico City, as long as you plan accordingly.

So, here's what you need to know.

The first time I came to Mexico city, I was looking for a hotel with a rooftop pool...and then Emy corrected me and told me that it was way too cold to swim. Too cold?! But isn't this Mexico?

She corrected me. Yes, you're coming to Mexico but you're not coming to the tropics! Bring a sweater!

Mexico City's weather is defined as a "sub-tropical highland climate". Sounds exotic right? But this just means that summers are nice and warm while winters are mild. And while summer can be rainy, most of the year it's a really beautiful climate. You won't be sweating your ass off all day. Instead, you'll experience sunny mornings, crisp evenings, and some chilly nights.

A SEASONAL BREAKDOWN:

Spring: Most people consider spring to be the best time to visit Mexico City because the weather is nice, the skies are clear and the chance of rain is pretty low. You don't usually need to wear a jacket during the day, and at night, a light jacket will do. In short, the temps are pleasant. But the best part of coming to Mexico City in the spring? All the flowers are in full bloom and the whole city turns purple!

Summer: Still lovely weather...with the chance of showers in the afternoon. Rain showers usually come in the form of short downpours. Your best bet is to plan your outdoor activities in the morning and stick indoors in the afternoons. Rainy days in the city are such a vibe, though. The perfect time to duck into a cafe for coffee amongst other rain refugees. Embrace it. Maybe you'll meet the love of your life during a sudden downpour! Just don't forget your umbrella.

Fall: The rains continue as the city transitions from summer to fall, but the days start getting shorter and cooler. On this last leg of the rainy season (September), morning showers stay short. But in the afternoon, there can be downpours that last hours. As soon as October hits, however, rain becomes scarce and it becomes full-on sweater weather!

Winter: Dry, sunny days and chilly to cold nights. Some nights can even go down to below freezing. December is also a fun time to visit because the city is full of Christmas decorations, and the markets sell all kinds of seasonal snacks like "buñuelos" (a thin, fried large fritter sprinkled with syrup; see the Mexican Food guide on page 33) and warm punch. Pack a warm jacket for the evenings and you're all set.

Blah blah blah, I know. Here's what to expect in a nutshell.

"Official" Best Time To Visit:	March - May
Busiest Time To Visit:	March through June (though this city is always busy lately!)
High Season:	March - May
Low Season:	December - February/ June - August
Warmest Weather:	May - July
Coldest Weather:	November - January
Hottest Month:	April
Coldest Month:	January
Driest Month:	February
The Rainiest Month:	July

Alexa's Vote on the Best Time to Visit:

Spring (March - May):

And especially during "Semana Santa", Mexico's spring break because most locals flee the city to go on vacation, so you get to enjoy an emptier, calmer city than usual.

And Late October / Early November:

Not weather related…but coming to experience the Day of the Dead in Mexico City is totally worth it. The city is full of altars and everyone's colorful costumes. (See Festivals & Holidays in Mexico, page 260)

Emilia's Vote on the Best Time to Visit:

February…for Art Week! If you're an art / design lover, this is when you should come. Exhibits and events featuring artists from all over the world spread out all across town. Plus, the social scene is buzzing with so many parties and afterparties everywhere! More on this on page 263.

Got all that? Okay, next up…

Learn How to Travel Longer, Cheaper and Safer

Get The One-Way Ticket Plan, available in paperback, kindle and audio.

Get yours at Alexa-West.com ☞

Visas for Mexico

Start with a tourist visa.

What: A tourist visa allows you to stay in Mexico for 6 months as a tourist.

How: You just show up. No need to prepare a single document and it's free.

Tip: When you arrive in Mexico, you will fill out a declaration card that you will hand to immigration at the airport. Have the address of your hotel ready to write on your declaration card as proof that you're a tourist. Also, as long as you've read this book and have an idea of what fun things you want to do in Mexico, you'll be granted entry into Mexico easy-peasy.

Other Tip - Illustrated through Story (yay):

The first time I entered Mexico as a tourist, I heard that I could stay 6 months. So when immigration asked me how long I planned to be here, I said "I don't know…six months? I don't have a plan!". That was the wrong answer. Suspicious that I'd stay forever, the immigration lady stamped my passport so that I could only stay 3 months. What a buzzkill!

The lesson here, though, is to sound like you have a plan even if you don't. If you don't have a flight out yet, just express your intentions to leave in a month or let them know you're going to Puerto Vallarta next and plan to fly home after six months exactly. Just have some kind of a plan to tell immigration.

Mexican Food Guide

Have you ever been sad at a Mexican restaurant? No? That's because Mexican food is happy food - prepare to be happier than you've ever been because you're about to discover tons of Mexican food that you've never even heard of. I guarantee it.

The first time I ever traveled to Mexico with Emy, I was eating something totally new to me on a daily basis. I discovered that there is a whole world of Mexican food that us gringos have never tried. So in this section, Emilia is going to do for you what she did for me and take you on a deeper dive beyond the burrito! But not beyond the taco because it turns out that there are a billion ways to prepare and eat a taco...

TACOS

In case you've been living in a cult that doesn't allow fun and you've never had a taco, let me explain what a taco is. A taco is simply a tortilla that is folded to hold any kind of yumminess inside. The taco possibilities are literally endless but here's a quick glossary with some of the most common tacos you'll find (and the names to order them by).

Carne Asada: Beef on the grill. This is a level 1 taco. Easy, delicious.

Bistec: Bistec is a word that was born from "beef steak". What's the difference between bistec and asada? Bistec can be cooked in different ways, either grilled or in a stew. Whereas Asada literally means grilled, so it will always mean grilled meat and has no chance of being stewed meat.

Pastor: Spiced pork straightly cut off of a big spinning-top, shawarma-style. It's served with a slice of pineapple and crowned with cilantro and onion.

Pescado: Fish tacos! Mostly common in coastal areas. You can find either grilled or breaded fish either in a flour or corn tortilla.

Camaron: Shrimp tacos! Same as the fish, you can find grilled or breaded shrimp in a flour or corn tortilla.

Lengua: Tongue. Yes, you read correctly. A taco filled with cow's tongue. Believe it or not, the flavor is amazing. Especially when served with salsa verde (green sauce). Even Alexa eats this.

Carnitas: Pulled pork that can be either boiled or fried. Pro Tip: Asked for "maciza", the not-so-greasy part of the meat, plus maciza is free of skin chunks.

Cabeza: It literally means head, but a cabeza taco is actually cow's cheek or neck. It sounds weird but it's actually super soft and tender meat! If anything, try it so you can tell people back home that you've eaten Tacos de Cabeza.

Suadero: A thin cut of meat between the belly and the leg of a cow or a pork. You'll find it either confited or fried. This is a street food classic.

Costilla: Tacos filled with rib meat. Tender and soft and yummy.

Cecina: Thin meat that has been marinated and salted to then be dried either in the air and sun or smoked. While cecina isn't as soft to bite, it's very flavorful and worth the try!

Chicharron: Chicharron is not only the best way to practice rolling those "r"s when ordering! It's also quite delicious. Made of seasoned and fried pork belly, skin, or rinds, you can find Chicharron soft or crunchy, as a dish itself or as a snack. But you'll mostly see it inside tacos!

What's the difference between chicharron and pork rinds? Pork rinds are made only from skin whereas chicharrones often consist of fat and some meat as well.

Guisados: Guisados are stews made with veggies, seafood, chicken, beef, or pork. Many things can be considered a guisado in Mexico, but in tacos, you'll most commonly find things like shredded chicken in a salsa verde or rajas con crema (slices of chile poblano with a creamy sauce). You're most likely to find tacos de guisado in very local spots.

Tacos Sudados or Tacos de Canasta: This translates as "sweaty tacos," and it's because these tacos sweat when they are steamed. They are small, super soft tacos usually filled with potatoes, chorizo, beans, and other stuff. They are also called Tacos de Canasta, Basket Tacos because they are all put inside a basket and covered with a cloth to keep them warm. You'll see people with these baskets selling these tacos on the street.

Other peculiar taco fillings: In the taco world, you will also come across tripa (intestines), seso (brains), and ojo (eyes). If you want to channel your inner Anthony Bourdain, go for it. But if you're on the more introverted side of the foodie spectrum, I'd avoid these at all costs.

And now that you're a taco expert…let's continue on our Mexican food

SAFE TUMMY TIP! In Mexico City, you will only find Seafood tacos in trendy or fancy restaurants, rarely on the streets. And if you do find fish street tacos, run away. Fish is always more delicate than beef, chicken or pork, so eating fish on the street is risky. Save the street food fish tacos for when you visit coastal Mexican cities.

LOCAL TIP! "You know a taco stand is good when it's full…but full of women. Women won't waste calories on a lousy taco."
- ASTRID, FROM EATLIKEALOCAL.MX

TORTILLAS, TORTILLAS AND MORE TORTILLAS...

First, a note about tortillas...because tortillas go way beyond tacos. Tortillas are the base of Mexican cooking, they are to us what bread is to Americans and Europeans. They are not only used to prepare many, many dishes but to accompany almost every meal. There are Mexicans that will simply not eat without a tortilla, whatever it is they are eating. Tortillas are freshly brought every single day from "tortillerías" small shops dedicated to making and selling tortillas.

During your stay in Mexico, you'll see your regular yellow corn tortilla but also blue-corn tortillas and, of course, flour tortillas. These are some of the tortilla-based dishes you'll get to try during your trip:

Quesadilla: Take a taco and add cheese. A tortilla folded or two tortillas stacked filled with cheese which are grilled and melted together. But guess what! In Mexico, a quesadilla doesn't always have cheese! Especially in Mexico City, if you want a cheesy quesadilla, you'll have to order a "quesadilla con queso". What's the difference between cheese-less quesadillas and tacos? Not even we Mexicans know. It's a nationwide debate.

Sincronizada: A quesadilla filled with ham. Simple and delicious. We usually eat these for dinner or supper.

Gringa: A Gringa is a quesadilla reloaded: a quesadilla filled with meat. Most commonly pastor or carne asada, and they're HEAVEN.

Burritos: Burritos aren't as common in Mexico as you'd think. They were originally invented for Americans. The further South you go, the less you'll find 'em. Burritos are characterized as flour tortillas rolled and wrapped around yummy fillings like beef, chicken, eggs...you name it.

Real Mexican burritos, though, rarely include rice or all of that other shit you find at Chipotle. Most burritos here are simpler, they will be stuffed with beans and cheese, machaca (fried beef), or some kind of stew. Burritos are often sold at roadside stands for road-trippers. They are almost as thin and dainty as taquitos, just not fried. It's the perfect handheld driving food.

FUN FACT! Burrito translates as "little donkey". Burro to burrito!

Chilaquiles: Believe it or not... chilaquiles are a breakfast dish. And in this Mexican's opinion...the best thing we Mexicans have ever created. You take tortilla chips, fry them and salsa and simmer them together. This is a dish invented out of leftovers, it's what Mexicans do with day-old tortillas. You'll find chilaquiles offered both soft and crunchy and topped with either red or green salsa. You can customize your chilaquiles, too. Most often, you'll order them plain, with shredded chicken, or with a fried egg on top. Pro Tip: Order them "divorciados" (divorced) which means you'll get half with red salsa and half with green salsa.

FUN FACT: Chilaquiles (chil-a-kill-layes) is Alexa's favorite G-rated word in the Spanish language. This word, chilaquiles, comes from the Aztec's Nahuatl language meaning chilis and greens.

Enchiladas: You probably know enchiladas if you grew up in the US, but if you don't, they go like this: rolled tortillas stuffed with meat like chicken or beef, and topped with sauce, cream and onions.

Gorditas: Gordita is a "sweet" way to call someone or something chubby. In this case, a tortilla. Gorditas are smaller in diameter than a tortilla and also thicker. They have a slit on one side (kind of like a pita pocket) where they are stuffed with cheese, meat, or some other filling, creating a savory pocket full of Mexican goodness.

Sopes: Fried masa base with different toppings like meat, chicken, veggies, and even seafood. It's similar to a tostada but smaller and with a mushier and fluffier base.

Tlacoyo: My favorite Mexican street food snack! You'll see little stands sprinkled all over the city where ladies are preparing tlacoyos right on the street. A blue corn tortilla filled with beans, chicharron, or requeson (a cheese similar to ricotta or cottage cheese) and served with some salsa, nopales (cactus), and a little bit of cheese sprinkled on top.

SNACKS & ENTREES

Guacamole: You know this one. And yes, it sometimes costs extra here too.

Queso Fundido: Don't be fooled, my Tex-mex princesses! When you order "queso" in Mexico, it's often not going to come out as a liquid easy for scooping with tortilla chips. This one takes a little more finagling.

Queso Fundido is melty cheese served on a hot plate that sometimes you need a fork to wrangle. Imagine the inside of a mozzarella stick served with mushrooms, or veggies, or chorizo (see below). This cheese will most commonly be served with tortillas ("para taquear") to make little tacos. So yeah, this is sold as an appetizer but it's its own event.

Nachos: You probably don't need me to explain nachos, but I will say this: even though nachos are Mexican, I'd dare say they are more common in the U.S. than they are in Mexico. But you will still find them here, and they will have real, gooey, molten cheese instead of the yellow salsa-like cheese the gringo version has.

STREET FOOD

Mexican food can be extremely casual. Many things you'll eat with your hands, and maybe even standing up next to a food stall. Here are some of them…

Tamales: If a sandwich and a burger had a baby, you'd get a torta. The foundation of this dish is meat, cheese, and veggies pressed between bread loaves called terms. But the fillings can vary so much that you could never eat the same torta twice. You can stuff a torta with carnitas, tamales and even chilaquiles. Keep reading to learn where to find the best tortas in the city.

Torta: If a sandwich and a burger had a baby, you'd get a torta. The foundation of this dish is meat, cheese, and veggies pressed between bread loaves called terms. But the fillings can vary so much that you could never eat the same torta twice. You can stuff a torta with carnitas, tamales and even chilaquiles. Keep reading to learn where to find the best tortas in the city.

Ps. In Spain, torta means cake. In Mexico, torta means sandwich.

Pambazos: A torta with pre-soaked bread in guajillo chili sauce, filled with chorizo, cream, potatoes, and queso fresco (fresh cheese).

Molletes: A slice of baguette-like bread smeared with beans and molten cheese on top. Simple, but delicious! Typically eaten for breakfast.

Esquites: An iconic street food snack. Boiled corn kernels in a cup topped with mayonnaise, lime, cotija cheese, and sprinkled with chili powder. It sounds weird, but I promise, it's delicious…as with so many things within the Mexican food universe.

Birria: Birria is not as widely known as other Mexican dishes. It is a stew made with meat (goat, mostly) and simmered slowly in a sauce and spices. And, of course…tacos. Biria isn't as common in Mexico City, but you'll still find some amazing birria tacos in some spots.

PRO TIP… Birria is one of the best things that can happen to you if you're hungover. You're welcome.

THINGS YOU WANT TO SIT DOWN FOR…

Mexican food can also be fancy and formal and require manners. These are dishes you're going to sit down for and take your time with.

Chiles Rellenos (Alexa's favorites): A big roasted green chili cut open, gutted, and stuffed with seasoned ground pork, covered with an egg white or corn batter and then bathed in salsa, of course.

Chiles en Nogada: Basically, Chiles Rellenos (see above) but fancier. They're filled with seasoned ground beef and topped with a white, creamy walnut sauce and pomegranate seeds. This dish was made to mimic the green, white, and red of the Mexican flag, and it's served around September when Mexico's Independence Day is celebrated…and when pomegranate season is in full swing.

Mole: Mole (pronounced mo-lay) is one of the most iconic Mexican dishes. It takes over 30 ingredients to prepare, starting with several kinds of chili and ingredients like nuts and cacao. Mole is a marinade and a sauce used to bathe meat like chicken or beef. There are around seven types of mole, but the most popular one is the "Poblano" (from Puebla). Some people say that mole has a subtle chocolatey taste to it, by the way, because one of the ingredients is cacao!

FUN FACT! Mole is an ancient word for "mix".

PRO TIP! One of Mexico's most famous Moles is chef Enrique Olvera's "Mole Madre", which is a plate of nothing but "Mole Viejo" ancient Mole that has been cooked uninterruptedly for over 2,000 days (at the time this book was written). And on top, a spoonful of fresh "Nuevo Mole".

Pozole: A traditional Mexican stew made with hominy (whole kernels of dried field corn), meat, and many, many seasonings. Topped with different elements like onions, cilantro, cabbage, chilies, etc. This is like grandma's home-cookin'.

Tostadas: A hard tortilla shell topped with a mix of either seafood or shredded chicken/meat and veggies. Both totally different dishes, but both are insanely good. Rumored to be invented over 2,000 years ago in Oaxaca.

Ceviche: The recipe for ceviche varies from beach to beach, but the base remains the same: raw fish, onion, tomato, chiles, cilantro, and lime. The citrus cooks the fish and makes it ready for eating. It's made to be eaten with corn chips and some "salsa marisquera" (spicy salsa made for seafood). And because there is no beach in Mexico City, expect chaos with ceviche variations around every corner.

PRO TIP! Take a tostada and smear it with some mayo. Put the ceviche on top. Take a bite. Bonus points for extra avocado on top.

TOPPINGS & OTHER SURPRISES

Chorizo: Mexican spicy pork sausage that is fermented, smoked, and cured. It's usually used as an accompaniment to other dishes like scrambled eggs, queso fundido, enchiladas, etc. Or it can be the main star in things like tacos!

Escamoles: Yep, another insect. Escamoles are insect caviar, or most commonly ants. They're super tasty, with a buttery-nutty taste. However, it's one of those things you can get food poisoning easily. So I tend to avoid them unless I'm at a place I completely trust. Like a high-end dining experience that knows what they're doing (the restaurant Expendio de Maiz uses them, and they're yummy).

Flor de Calabaza: Squash sprouts are sauteed and commonly used as a taco or quesadilla fillings. But now they are showing up in many different forms on menus across town. They're delicious and a great veggie alternative!

Chapulines: Not a dish, but an ingredient you might run into often while in Mexico City. Chapulines are grasshoppers! Yes, crispy, crunchy grasshoppers that have been sauteed either naturally or spiced. They've become a fashionable ingredient, and they will make an appearance on many menus in Mexico City. But you can also buy them by themselves in markets or with street vendors. Add some lime and chili, and you've got a super healthy mid-morning snack. Seriously, they're full of protein!

♥ **Alexa here.** Hi. Just stopped by to say that I have indeed witnessed Emilia order a full bag of chapulines from a vendor and then proceed to walk around the market eating them like they're peanuts. I'm not there yet, but I do love to steal a couple for myself on occasion.

PRO TIP! In Mexico, chips are called "totopos"!

SALSAS

Salsas can come in so many colors, textures, flavors, and, most importantly, levels of spiciness. You have them mild, medium, spicy and crazy, and killer hot. The trick is to always do a salsa test before putting any on your plate. Put a drop on the back of your hand and try. You can also always or server: "Picante?" but know that if they say no, there's a chance that it will still be a little bit spicy. My rule of thumb is this:

☞ If a server says it isn't spicy, it will be a little spicy.

☞ If they say it's going to be a little spicy, then it's definitely going to be spicy.

Here are five basic salsas you'll definitely run into while you're in Mexico:

Salsa Mexicana, aka Pico de Gallo: Probably the best-known Mexican salsa. This is an easy one, consisting of just diced tomato, onion, garlic, cilantro, and jalapeños, add some lime, and that's it. It's often served as an appetizer with tortilla chips to wait while your food is served.

Salsa Verde: This is one of my favorite salsas because it tends to be on the milder side and because it has a lemony zest to it. It's made of cooked tomatillos, jalapeños, cilantro, onions, garlic, and lime. It's a fresh salsa used for many dishes, like chicharrón and chilaquiles. But you can add to anything you'd like.

Salsa Roja de Molcajete: Tomatoes, serrano peppers, and garlic are roasted to the point of blackened and blistered, and once they're so soft, grounded in a molcajete, a traditional volcanic stone mortar. This salsa is also usually mild too and has a rich and smokey flavor. This one is great for tacos, especially beef ones!

Salsa Taquera: A salsa made for tacos! It's made with tomatoes, green tomatillos, garlic, onion, and dried "chile de Arbol" that have been roasted, smashed, and blended, resulting in a light yet slightly smoky salsa that will make your tacos even better. This one can be spicy or not; better ask or try first!

Salsa Chipotle: Did you know Chipotles are just jalapeños that have been roasted and dried? Now you do! Add tomatoes, garlic, and onions and you've got a Salsa Chipotle. You'll find this one either smooth and blended or chunky, and since it's not usually very spicy, it goes great with almost everything!!

Tajín: Not technically a salsa, but still in the spicy condiment spectrum. Tajin is a brand of powdered, dried chilis that's become an actual term. It's sprinkled on top of fruit and snacks like watermelon, mango, coconut, cucumber, and jícama.

FUN FACT: In Mexican beaches, you'll often find that coconuts are opened up and the meat is eaten with lime, salt, and some chillies like Tajin. Try it. Your life will never be the same.

MEXICAN PRO TIP! Even though I'm Mexican, I'm the worst at handling spicy food. So, if you're like me, and you ever find yourself with your mouth on fire...eat some mayonnaise. It'll fix you right up.

BONUS! WANT TO TAKE SOME SALSAS HOME?

If you want to take any salsas home, I always recommend two: Salsa Cholula, because it's mildly spicy and has a delicious lemony taste. And Salsa Don Emilio, an oily salsa with dried chilies and seeds. This one can be super spicy, but you just add a couple tiny drops to give whatever you're eating an amazing kick. You can find both at Walmart in Mexico City, or preferably, many local convenience stores.

SWEETS

Flan: A baked custard dessert covered with a light caramel sauce. You may also find "choco-flan," a chocolate variation of flan.

Arroz con Leche: Sweet rice pudding made with milk evaporated milk and sweetened condensed milk. Sometimes you'll find a cinnamon stick in it, or ground cinnamon sprinkled on top. This is a must-try while you're here in Mexico!

Churros: Churros were inherited to Mexico from Spain, but they've become the staple dessert in Mexican cuisine. They are sweet, deep-fried dough snacks sprinkled with sugar and cinnamon and filled with caramel or chocolate. Or to be dipped in "chocolate caliente" (hot chocolate).

Pan Dulce: Pan Dulce encompasses a mix of Mexican pastries. The most iconic ones are Conchas, a fluffy bread with a sugary, patterned topping that resembles a turtle's shell. There's no exact definition of which pastries are considered Pan Dulce, but some of the most common ones are bisquets, trenzas, donuts, moños, and my favorites: puerquitos, little pigs, pastries shaped like pigs that are perfectly sweet, soft inside and brown outside.

Pan de Muerto: A sweet bread prepared for the Day of the Dead. You will only find this during October and early November. And no, even though it means Bread of the Dead, there's nothing weird about it, I promise. It's really delicious, and I'm always excited when Pan de Muerto season is around the corner.

PAN DE MUERTO SEASON IS THE BEST SEASON / 📷 @ STRIKING.FOOD

ALCOHOLIC DRINKS

Michelada: Micheladas are a whole different debate because you'll get something different depending on where you are. The basic Michelada is a beer with lime and salt. But in some places, it also means Worcestershire sauce and Tabasco. And in some others, it even has Clamato (tomato and clam juice). Ask before you order, but here is the quick guide to ordering these drinks in Mexico City:

→ **Michelada:** lime and salt

→ **Cubana:** lime, salt, Worcestershire sauce & Tabasco

→ **Cielo Rojo (red sky):** lime, salt, Worcestershire sauce, Tabasco & Clamato (clam and tomato juice)

Tequila: Mexico's most iconic drink...and probably even the most iconic word. Tequila is made from one specific kind of Blue Agave, which goes through a lengthy process of cooking, fermentation, and distillation. You can drink it straight or mixed in cocktails.

Margarita: The staple Mexican cocktail, it's prepared with tequila, orange liqueur, and lime juice. Served with salt on the rim of the glass and either shaken or blended.

Mezcal: Mezcal is Tequila's cousin, as they both come from agave. However, Tequila can only come from one kind of agave, while mezcal comes from over 20 types of agave. Mezcal is clear-colored, and its notes can go from spicy to smokey.

Raicilla: A cousin of mezcal and tequila, Raicilla is another distilled from agave that is about 300 years old. Raicilla is made from the roots of the agave and goes through a single-distilled process. It's usually fresh and crisp to the tongue and softer than you'd imagine. Once considered a humble drink because it was originally drunk by farmers, Raicilla is nowadays the up-and-coming spirit in Mexico.

TEQUILA FUN FACT... Tequila is named after a town named, you guessed it, Tequila in central Mexico. If it's not produced in the area, it cannot bear the name of Tequila and has to be labeled as "Destilado de Agave" (distilled from agave).

Carajillo: Allow me to introduce you to your new favorite drink. A carajillo consists of espresso and a shot of Licor 43, a sweet, citrusy Spanish liquor poured over ice. This drink is like a boozy dessert in a glass. It's usually served after meals as a digestif. But you can drink it at any time, and it's a wonderful pick-me-up to keep on sight-seeing through your afternoon. In some places, you'll find some alternate Carajillo versions served with Kahlua or Brandy.

NON-ALCOHOLIC DRINKS

Aguas Frescas: These non-alcoholic drinks are made with fruits like tamarind and flowers like hibiscus (Jamaica). One of the most common is Horchata, made of rice, milk, and cinnamon. You'll often find these at taco stands. I always recommend trying the Agua Fresca, no matter where you go.

Cafe de Olla: A traditional coffee beverage. It's black coffee with cinnamon and sweetened with "piloncillo" (unrefined whole cane sugar). Cafe de olla needs to be prepared in a clay pot (olla = pot) as it gives a special taste to the coffee. It is commonly served in tiny clay mugs as well.

Chocolate Caliente: Mexican hot chocolate is different from any you've ever tried. What makes it special? Spices like cinnamon and nutmeg in the mix. Besides, every hot chocolate can be different, and sometimes people will even add a dash of chili to it. No worries, it doesn't make it spicy, but it makes the flavors way more intense.

Atole: A warm heavy drink made with corn, masa (dough), and piloncillo (cane sugar). It's mostly drunk around the Day of the Dead and Christmas season. You'll find atole sold on many street corners around the city and the consistency varies from porridge-like to thin and watery.

Champurrado: All of the above but adding chocolate to the mix. Both these drinks are usually served to accompany tamales, but just the drink itself feels like a full meal.

And that's it!

Keep in mind this was just a "quick" food guide to cover most of the bites you'll encounter in Mexico City…but Mexican food in Mexico expands far beyond what's covered here. To show you every regional delight, we'd need a book of its own!

Hey, maybe that's a good idea. Should we write a Guide to Mexican Food next?! Let us know what you think at @sologirlstravelguide and @__helloemilia ♥

LOCAL MEXICAN TIP!

What Mexican dish do you HAVE to try in Mexico?

"Suadero Tacos and Pozole" — Wendy, a local girl from Mexico City who grew up inside the markets and is now a food tour guide for EatLikeALocal.

✎ **TRAVEL NOTES:**

....

....

....

....

....

....

Spanish Language Guide

Welcome to Mexican Spanish 101. Emphasis on the Mexican because words and phrases can vary greatly between Mexico, Spain, and Latin America in general.

In this section, you'll find useful phrases to help you navigate your time in Mexico. And even some slang words and phrases, so you sound like a local, not like a total tourist.

NOTE: words marked with a* are to be used with friends and never towards someone in a position of respect!

But first, here are some pronunciation tips from a Mexican...

How to not pronounce like a gringo...

Vowels are key. Vowels in Spanish are pretty much the same all the time.

A is always like the **"a"** in **father.**

E is always like the **"e"** in **bet.**

I is always like the **"i"** in **dinner.**

O is always like the **"o"** in **phone.**

U is always like the **"oo"** in **spoon**...unless it comes after a q or a g, in that case it becomes silent, like in quiero (pronounced kee-eh-roh).

If English is your native language, then you gotta fight your instincts a little bit. Spanish rarely has the "ow" sound at the end, unlike most people believe. We say "quiero" (kee-eh-roh) not "quiero" (kee-eh-row).

Got it? Okay, let's practice. Repeat after me...

→ **Chilaquiles:** chee- lah - kee - les

→ **Mexico:** meh-hee-koh

→ **Amigo:** Ah - mee - goh

→ **Gracias:** Grah - cee - ahs

→ **Turibus:** Too - ree - boos

→ **Museo:** Moo - seh - oh

→ **Mercado:** Mer - kah - doh

→ **Xochimilco:** Soh - chee - milk - oh

→ **Teotihuacan:** Teh - oh - tee - wah - can

And finally, don't even worry about sounding foolish at times. We all sound silly at first when learning a new or foreign language. Locals will always be super grateful and extra-friendly when someone tries to speak their own language. Have fun, and don't overthink it.

- EMILIA

GREETINGS

Hello	Hola! / Buenas!
My name is _____	Mi nombre es _____
Nice to meet you...	Mucho gusto / Encantado/a
Likewise	Igualmente
How are you?	Como estas? / Como andas?
What's up?	Que pasó? / Que onda?
What are you up to? What are you doing?	Que pedo?* / Que haces?

49

Good morning	Buenos días
Good afternoon	Buenas tardes
Good evening / night	Buenas tardes / Buenas noches
Thank you	Gracias
You're welcome	Denada / No hay de que
Good´-bye	Adios
See you later	Nos vemos

* You'll hear the word "pedo" a lot. It means, ahem, fart. So it doesn't make any sense, I know, but Mexicans use it for so many things in many ways, like "Vamos de peda", let's go get drunk.

It's total slang and not a very "proper" word to use. I would not use it in front of Emy's mom, for example. But we include it here, so you understand when you hear it.

DAY TO DAY

Yes	Si
No	No
Can I _____?	Puedo _____-?
No problem	No hay problema / Sin problema
I don't know / No idea	No se / Ni idea
I am finished	Terminé
What's this?	Que es esto?
Great	Muy bien!
I'm sorry	Lo siento! / Perdon!
Excuse me...	Disculpa...
Please	Por Favor / Porfa
I'm hungry / I'm starving	Tengo hambre / Tengo mucha hambre
I'm thirsty	Tengo sed

SHOPPING / ORDERING

Do you have ____?	Tienes ____?
How much...	Cuanto...
How many	Cuantos / Cuantas
People	Personas
How many people	Cuantas personas
I want...	Quiero
I don't want...	No quiero
Big	Grande
Small	Chico /Pequeño
Hot	Caliente
Cold	Frio
I like	Me gusta
I don't like	No me gusta
Do you have change?	Tienes cambio?
The check, please.	La cuenta, porfavor.
One more, please.	Uno mas, porfavor.
The menu	el menu / la carta

FOOD & DRINK

PRO TIP! Call your server male "joven" (pronounced ho-ven), instead of "señor". If it's a lady, you can call her "señorita". - Emilia

Food / Meal	Comida
Fast Food / Junk Food	Comida rapida
Street Food	Comida callejera
Water	Agua
Sparkling Water	Agua mineral
Ice	Hielo

Drink	Bebida
Cafe	Cafe
Tea	Te
Beer	Cerveza
Red Wine / White Wine	Vino Tinto / Vino Blanco
Delicious	Delicioso
Corn	Maiz
Avocado	Aguacate
Vegetables	Verduras / Vegetales
Juice	Jugo
Chicken	Pollo
Pork	Cerdo / Puerco
Beef	Carne / Res
Shrimp	Camaron
Fish	Pescado
Octopus	Pulpo
Tofu	Tofu
Vegetarian	Vegetariano
Vegan	Vegano
Fruit	Fruta
Rice	Arroz
Beans	Fijoles
Spicy / Not Spicy	Picante / No Picante

PRO TIP! Rolling your r's is a big part of speaking Spanish. Bring the tip of your tongue to the roof of your mouth. Now blow some air strongly. Rrrrrrrrrrr. You're ready to order a burrito like a local.

USEFUL WORDS & PHRASES

Where?	Donde?
Where is the bathroom?	Donde esta el baño?
Room / Hotel Room	Habitacion / Habitacion de hotel
To	A
From	Desde
Tomorrow	Mañana
Yesterday	Ayer
Day	Dia
Week	Semana
Month	Mes
Year	Año
Weekend	Fin de Semana

EMERGENCY PHRASES

Go away	Alejate!
Help!	Ayuda!
Police!	Police!
Stop!	Stop!
Not Safe	No es seguro

Ps. Have any more pronunciation and language questions? Send me a voice message at @__helloemilia, and I'll send you one back to help you get it right.

What to Pack for Mexico City

Don't stress! As long as you have your passport, bank card and a decent backpack, you're ready for Mexico City. Anything you need or forget at home can be found here. So, no matter what you do or do not pack - you'll be just fine.

But let's take this opportunity to get organized now so you don't have to spend your vacation hunting for things you forgot.

Everything in this chapter can be found in my Mexico packing list on my blog, Alexa-West.com/Blog

First, out with the tropical clothes, and in with the city clothes! The key to dressing for Mexico City is light layers.

PRO TIP: Always carry a tote bag with you in Mexico City so you can easily shed or add your layer of the day (a light jacket, sweater or shawl will do).

OTHER PRO TIP: The last time I came to Mexico City was after a month at the beach. I didn't want to carry around my city clothes all month, so I saved room in my bag and budget to hit Zara and some local shops once I got to CDMX.

WHAT TO PACK

✓ PASSPORT WITH AT LEAST 6 MONTHS VALIDITY

Some countries enforce it and some countries don't – but to play it safe, you need to have at least 6 months validity on your passport. For example, if it's January 1st, 2024, and your passport expires before June 1st, 2024, they might not let you in the country and you'll have to return home immediately.

✓ TRAVEL INSURANCE

Yes, you do need it. Everything from minor bouts of food poisoning to helicopter medevac off a mountain, a standard travel insurance policy is a non-negotiable in my (literal) book. Check your current medical insurance plan. They might already cover Mexico. If they don't, here is what I use:

 ✈ **World Nomads** which offers full-coverage plans for extremely reasonable prices.

✈ **SafetyWing** is also a really affordable option, especially if you're traveling long term.

✓ EMERGENCY MONEY SOURCE / $100 CASH US

Have a secret stash of cash and a backup credit card in case you get in a sticky situation. Keep this emergency money source separate from your other cards and cash so that if you lose your wallet, you won't lose the secret stash, too.

✓ BANK CARDS

Travel with two cards – either 2 debit cards or 1 debit + 1 credit. In the case that your bank flags one card with fraudulent activity and disables it, you'll want to have a backup. If the machine eats a card, if a card gets stolen, or if you lose your purse on a night out, a backup card will make all the difference between having mom fly you home and you continuing your travels.

NOTE! If you are from the UK, check out Starling Bank. They have the best atm exchange rates and don't charge any foreign atm charges. They can also send you a replacement if you lose or break your card to anywhere in the world that has an address!

✓ THE PERFECT BACKPACK OR SUITCASE

The Bag I Recommend…

The Osprey Farpoint 40 Litre Backpack ☞

It's been over 5 years that I've been using this bag. I love it so much that I just bought the exact same model again to use for another 5 years.

♥ This bag qualifies as a carry-on

♥ It's extremely comfortable to wear

♥ The open-zip style means that you can keep your clothes organized

♥ I swear it's got Mary Poppins magic because I can fit 3 months of clothes in one tiny space

 Or the **Osprey Fairview 55** that comes with a zip-on and off day bag.

✓ WALKING SHOES

Bring 3 pairs of shoes:

◊ 1 Pair of Flip Flops or Slides

◊ 1 Pair of Cute Walking Sandals

◊ 1 Pair of Hiking / Running Shoes

This is my official trifecta of shoes. Through rain, up mountains, and on long sweaty walks, they've never failed me. I replace the same pairs of shoes every year – find them in my Amazon Storefront.

✓ COLLAPSIBLE UMBRELLA

Especially if you're coming to Mexico City in the summer. A collapsible umbrella can permanently live in your bag without taking too much space and can be a life saver for an afternoon unannounced downpour.

✓ A TOTE BAG TO STASH YOUR EXTRA LAYERS

And that guava roll you'll probably buy for later. I always carry a folded or rolled up tote bag in my backpack or my bag in case I need to carry any extra stuff.

Want to make friends while you travel? Travel with one of our official tote bags which you can get in my Travel Shop.

✓ TROPICAL WEATHER MAKEUP

Humidity is no joke. Most foundations get super greasy and eye-shadows crease like it's their job. My makeup bag is pure perfection when it comes to long-lasting, humid, tropical weather products. Check out my travel makeup collection here.

✓ QUICK DRY TOWEL

Hostel girls! Hostels usually don't provide towels so it's nice to bring a travel towel of your own. Not a total necessity, but a quick dry (usually some kind of microfiber) towel is nice to have– especially during the rainy season when the heat isn't there to dry things quickly. Plus, it can double as your beach towel!

✓ ELECTRIC ADAPTER
Your phone and laptop are likely not going to be compatible with the Mexico outlets. REI, Target, and Amazon have cheap Universal adapters that every traveler should own. But don't worry, voltage is the same as in the US!

✓ MONEY CONCEAL POUCH

This credit card size pouch is used to discreetly carry cash, cards, and keys. The Velcro strap makes it easy to secure the pouch to your bra or undies for nights out on the town.

✓ EMPTY SPACE IN YOUR BAG

It took me 5 years to learn that the less stuff you have, the more free you are. You are free to pick up and move around, free to shop for souvenirs, and free from relying on porters and taxis to help you carry your luggage. Plus, you're going to need space for all that extra shopping over here.

WHAT NOT TO PACK

✗ High Heels - Mexico City is a fashion mecca, but I'd save space in my bag for other stuff. You'll be walking a lot so bring some fancy flats instead.

✗ A Pharmacy of Medicine - You can get it all here!

✗ Tropical Clothes Only - If you're headed somewhere beachy before or after Mexico City, don't forget to pack some light layers to pile on.

Check out the rest of **my Travel Essentials** in my Amazon Storefront here ➔

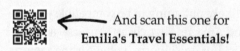
⬅— And scan this one for **Emilia's Travel Essentials!**

How to Budget for Mexico City

How much money should I bring?

How much will I spend? What is the least amount I can spend and still see it all?

When it comes to traveling Mexico, there are 3 spending routes you can take:

BUDGET 💸

Stay in hostels, eat local, take the super convenient minibus, and drink beer from 7-Eleven.

BALANCED 💸 💸

Spend the night in a hostel and eat street food one night, then check into a cute boutique hotel and treat yourself to dinner! Or just stay middle of the road the whole way through—not too fancy but comfortable.

BOUGIE 💸 💸 💸

Luxury hotels, top-notch tasting menus, private tours, and some fun shopping.

	BUDGET	BALANCED	BOUGIE
TOTAL PER DAY	$30	$80	$160+

All 3 of these options are possible, easy, and will offer you the trip of a lifetime – as long as you plan it right.

Here are some breakdowns of the costs you can expect to spend on CDMX.

Street Taco	$.5 - $1
Restaurant Meal	From $15-20
McDonald's	$4.75
Bottle of Beer	$1.50 store / $3 bars
Capuccino	$3
1 Night in a Hostel	$20
1 Night in a Basic AirBnb (low season)	$60+
1 Night in a Basic AirBnb (high season)	$100.00+
1 Night in a Boutique Hotel	$100-$350
1 Hour Massage	$40
1 30 min. Uber ride (non-peak hours)	$7.50

On a budget? Tips to spend less in Mexico City...

→ Visit during "low season" when hotels are 30-50% cheaper

→ Go to the ATM just once a week – the ATM fees can be up to $8 per transaction

→ Drink beer from mini marts or hole in the wall bars, rather than clubs

→ Take the bus and go on DIY adventures

→ Eat street food

Your biggest expenses will be...

💸 Alcohol

💸 Organized Tours

💸 Ubers and Drivers

Everything else can be tweaked to fit your wallet.

Tipping is customary. The average is a 15% tip, but if your service was nothing special, then people tip 10%. Anything below 10% is usually considered cheap. Unless, of course, your service was a nightmare and ruined your dinner. It's also recommended to tip your salon ladies at the end of a service. Service will rarely be included in the bill, but it sometimes happens in more touristic spots.

☞"La propina está incluida?" (Is the tip included?) to make sure.

Paying with a card but want to tip? You don't just sign the bill with your tip after they've ran the card. You've got to tell them what you want to tip. This is how you do it in Mexico City. When the waiter brings the credit card machine thingy, hand them your card and ask them to add 10% (or whatever) and they'll add it on automatically.

Let's Talk About Money in Mexico City

You're going to need cash in Mexico!

Hotels and big restaurants may accept cards, but street food, transportation and haggling on anything requires cash-ola!

How much money to bring to Mexico:
$0 USD to spend - $100 USD emergency cash

Use the ATMs instead of the exchange counters. ATMs usually give you the market exchange rate. But here's a pro tip: If the ATM asks you "do you want to accept the bank's conversion" click on "decline conversion".

I suppose: If you are super pro-active and excited, you can exchange USD/your currency for pesos at your local bank at home. Just double check that their exchange rates are close to the official market's exchange rates (at a bank, they should be accurate).

WHAT YOU NEED TO KNOW ABOUT MONEY IN MEXICO...

Mexican currency is called **pesos.**

A Quick Tip to Converting US dollars to Pesos with your Brain:

Take the number in pesos, cut it in half and take away a zero. Like this.

→ 2,000 pesos = 100 USD

→ 100 pesos = 5 USD

→ 50 pesos = $2.5 USD

Getting Local Currency...

When you land in Mexico, I recommend taking 2000-5000 ($100 - $250 USD) pesos out of the ATM depending on your plans. This way you avoid being charged the ATM fees over and over again.

Which ATMs to Use in Mexico?

Always use a bank-affiliated ATM (i.e. a bank-branded ATM instead of a weird generic ATM). You get the best exchange rate at official Bank ATM machines!

Alexa-Approved ATMs:

✓ Banco Azteca charges a flat 30-pesos ($2 USD) fee plus your bank fee.

✓ Santander and Banamex offer great fees and fair exchange rates, as well.

ATMs I Avoid:

✗ Tangerine and Scotiabank. They charge 12% conversion rates. That's high!

⚠ ATM REMINDER: Sometimes, ATMs spit out your money first and your card second, resulting in many forgotten cards! Do a 3-step check before you leave: cash, card, receipt.

MONEY SAVING TIP: In Mexico, ATMs will often ask you, "Do you want to use the ATM exchange rate?" Hit decline! DECLINE THE ATM EXCHANGE RATE, which charges another 5% conversion. You want the default market exchange rage.

Market Exchange rate = good

Bank/ATM Exchange rate = manipulated

"Decline Conversion" at ATMs won't mean you receive no money. It just means that you'll get the rate your bank is offering, rather than one that may be a lot higher. So always decline!

CARDS YOU SHOULD BE TRAVELING WITH

My # 1 Travel Rule: Don't book your flight and hotels with a debit card!

☞ **Reason #1:** If your flight or trip is cancelled, you will have no trip protection and you may never see your cash again.

☞ **Reason #2:** You are literally turning down free money if you're not taking advantage of travel credit card points when booking international flights and weeks of hotels.

Use a Travel Credit Card to...

◊ Book your flight

◊ Book your hotels

◊ Pay at restaurants

What About Debit Cards?

FOR AMERICANS, open an account with Charles Schwab Bank. With Charles Schwab, I can use any ATM in the world without ATM fees.

Every time you use an ATM that isn't your bank's ATM, you are charged a "foreign ATM fee" that can be $3–8 depending on where you are. Lame. But at the end of every month, Charles Schwab reimburses all foreign ATM fees.

Are you in the military? USAA also offers this "no ATM fee" service!

Internet & Data in Mexico

Almost everywhere you go, Mexico City will have WiFi; there's even free wifi in many public spaces. But what about the places in between, like when you're catching an Uber outside of a restaurant, in a car headed to a new city, walking, and getting lost? You need cell phone data, mija.

Just Visiting?

Get a SIM card when you land in Mexico.

In Mexico, I used a company called Telcel for my internet data.

How Much: The SIM card (the little chip they will put in your phone) was 300 pesos ($15 USD) and I pay around 200 pesos a month($10) for internet on my phone.

Where to Get It:

→ Inside the Airport at the Oxxo (there are a few). Or at any Oxxo around town.

→ In town. Just put "Telcel" in your google maps and you'll find a location where you can buy the SIM card. The malls have Telcel kiosks, too.

To "top up" (add more internet on your card when you run out), you can go into an OXXO mini-mart, tell them "200 pesos Telcel", give them your phone number, and they will top up for you in a couple of minutes time. And don't worry about where to find an OXXO. You'll see them everywhere!

IMPORTANT: To use a Mexican data plan, please make sure your phone is "Unlocked." This means that you can use other companies' data plans. You can just go to your cell carrier's store, hand them the phone and say, "I need this unlocked," and they should do it for you on the spot. If not, message me on Instagram, and I'll give you some pointers > @sologirlstravelguide

PRO TIP FOR AMERICANS AND CANADIANS: Your cell phone plan might already cover Mexico! Double check now. And hey, consider switching to Google Fi if you travel often. It's the plan I use in the states and abroad (even in Thailand and Bali).

Don't Get an "International Plan" on top of your current plan. That plan is expensive and doesn't guarantee good coverage. Besides! Mexican cell phone data is cheap, easy to get, and has great coverage.

APPS TO DOWNLOAD FOR MEXICO CITY

WhatsApp:

The main messaging app and calling app out here. It's free to call and text whenever you have an internet connection (Wi-Fi or cell data).

Uber, Didi, Beat

Just like at home. Connect your credit card inside the Uber App so you don't have to handle cash.

InDriver

Like Uber, I use InDriver nearly every day. They provide an Uber-style service with a bidding-system.

UberEats, Rappi & DidiFood

All the food delivery you could need especially on those days you're too tired from having so much fun while you explore. UberEats and Rappi also have shopping options so you can even get your groceries, and basically anything you need, delivered right to your door.

PRO TIP: many restaurants have a WhatsApp number where they take food orders and deliver for free or for cheap. Check their Facebook page or Instagram!

Google Maps Offline

This is a life saver when you don't have access to Wi-Fi. You can save Google Maps offline area-by-area. So open "Puerto Vallarta" on your Google Maps, type "Puerto Vallarta" (or any other area) and click "download". Now you can access the map without the internet.

Mexico City Metro Map App

The App you need for easier navigation through Mexico City's subway.

Moovit

An app that shows you viable public transportations routes considering the metro, metrobus and buses. It also alerts you on any delays or changes on the routes. The downside is that this app doesn't work offline.

XE

Currency Conversions in an instant so that you don't get ripped off while buying a cute hat at the market!

Accuweather

The most reliable weather app out there. Especially useful during the rainy season!

SkyAlert

Don't freak out, but Mexico City is an earthquake zone. So if you're staying for a longer period of time, this is a must-have app. SkyAlert is a natural disaster warning system that can let you know up to 60 seconds before an earthquake.

PRO TIP! For more info on what to do in case of an earthquake, go to the "What Do in Case of…" section towards the end of this book.

Bumble and Tinder

Find a sightseeing partner with another traveler or link up with a local who knows all the best spots in the city. Mexico City is very pro-dating app.

Fun Fact: Bumble has a friend-mode called Bumble BFF where you can search for new friends to explore with!

Duolingo

Start learning Spanish before you come!

Translate

While I encourage you to learn at least a little basic Spanish, iTranslate is a handy translating app that lets you translate on the spot.

MY FACEBOOK GROUPS TO JOIN

 The Solo Girl's Travel Community
where you can ask questions and meet other girls.

Girls in Mexico City
to find other girls traveling to or living in Mexico City

MY FACEBOOK PAGE

 The Solo Girl's Travel Guide
Follow and Like my Facebook page to see where I'm traveling next.

Transportation in Mexico

Mexico City is pretty walkable once you're within each neighborhood. And walking is the best way to experience what the city has to offer. You'll be able to walk within the microcosmos of each neighborhood or maybe even walk between neighboring areas if you're wearing the right shoes. However, for longer distances, rainy days, or once it gets late, you'll need other ways to move around.

PUBLIC TRANSPORTATION

METRO, AKA THE SUBWAY

The metro has 12 lines, 195 stations and it's used by 7.5 million people daily. Don't let this intimidate you. The lines are made for tourists and locals to be able to navigate. You can do this.

Oh, and this can be one hell of a crowded ride! But hey, guess what! There are female-only cars! That's right, train cars are just for girls. While this should make you feel more safe, you still have to take precautions. Don't stray too far from the neighborhoods I've mentioned in this book, and don't ride alone at night. Ps. Avoid peak hours to avoid the crowds. The metro is at its fullest between 6am to 9am, and 6pm to 9pm.

⊙ **Open:** The metro operates daily from 5am 'til midnight.

✐ **Budget:** $5 pesos per ride

METROBUS

The MetroBus is the newer and nicer version of the Metro. It's an above-the-ground system with 6 fixed routes. The MetroBus runs closer to Roma and Condesa. If you're staying in this area, this is a convenient option. You need a Card to use the MetroBus, but the same card works for both the Metro and the MetroBus.

How to get your MetroCard:

You can get your card directly at the machines in Metro stations or at the ticket booths. They can be sold out from time to time, so just check another booth within the same station. Or you can purchase a single-ride ticket and check again at the station where you arrive.

⊙ **Open:** 5am 'til midnight, but functioning times can vary according to each line. Check the specific times for each line in this code.

📎 **Budget:** $6 pesos per ride

PRO TIP! Download the Mexico City Metro Map app to plan your routes. And the Moovit app to get any notifications related to your routes.

Transportation to Avoid

There are other public transportation options available that are either not suitable for a solo travel girl or you just won't need, so let's take note of them below to avoid confusion when planning your routes:

✖ There's the Trolebus, a tram-like bus attached to cables. But you probably won't need it.

✖ Avoid the Local Buses or Peseros, they're harder to navigate and always crowded.

✖ The Tren Ligero only runs in the South of the city, while the Suburbano only in the North. You won't be going in these areas.

CARS & DRIVERS

For convenience, I usually use ride share services while visiting Mexico City. However, if you're staying here for a longer period of time, the cost does add up. Just keep that in mind. Ride share prices are a bit cheaper than in the US but not by much.

UBER

Being the most widely-known ride sharing app, Uber doesn't need an introduction. It's the go-to for many when it comes to transportation in Mexico City. However, with so many visitors in Mexico City post-pandemic, Uber prices are higher than usual lately so it's worth it to compare prices with these cheaper ride share apps below...

DIDI

Didi works just like Uber, but it's a tad cheaper. You can use DidiFood for delivery, too.

CABIFY

Cabify is the latin version of Uber, available in Spain and Latin America.

BEAT

Same as the ones before, but with shorter wait times. Plus, once in the app you can choose the BeatTesla option and have a Tesla (or Tesla-like cars) pick you up, you fancy thing.

SAFETY TIP! Always always always check the name and plates of the driver. And share your ETA with a friend when riding alone. You can do this in the apps. There's no such thing as being too careful!

BIKES & SCOOTERS

Cheaper than a car and more fun, too. When my route is too long to walk but too short to get a car, I love to make use of bikes and scooters in CDMX.

ECO BICI

You'll find EcoBici stations sprinkled around in most of the chapters in this book. This is such a fun and easy way to move around, especially for short distances. In some stations you'll find electric bikes as well.

🚲 Budget:

Bikes are $2 USD per hour, your first ever 45 minutes are free.

Day passes are $5 USD.

And there are longer memberships available if you're staying around for a while. A debit or credit card is required to sign-up.

ELECTRIC SCOOTERS

I prefer scooters over bikes, personally. There's a bunch of options of shared scooters around the city. Rates are fairly similar among them, so you can go with the one that you stumble upon...but here's a chart comparing the rates if you want to budget ahead:

	LIME	GRIN	BIRD	MOVO
Unlocking Fee	$10	$10	$20	$10
Fee per-minute	$3	$2	$2	$2
Hourly Rate	$190	$130	$140	$130

*ALL PRICES IN PESOS / LATEST RATES BY THE DATE OF PUBLISHING, WINTER 2022

PRO TIP! Grin includes 3 free minutes with its unlocking fee. Plus, it's the only one that's a Mexican start-up. So using GRIN = supporting the local community.

SAFETY TIP! If you're moving around on a scooter, stay away from big, heavy transit and high-speed streets.

ECONDUCE: ELECTRIC MOTOR BIKES

This is the newest way to move around Mexico City. Small electrical motorcycles that function just like all the ride-sharing scooters above. You just download the app, find your nearest ride and go. You can rent it monthly, or just pay for the minutes you use.

	Fare p/ min	Minutes Included	Monthly Fee	Minimum Charge	Full Day (9am-9pm)	Booking Fee
BASIC PLAN	$3.50	--	--	$50	--	$10 / 5 min
PRO PLAN	$3	60 min.	$249	$30	$250	$0 / 5 min
PREMIUM PLAN	$2	300 min.	$649	$15	$200	$0 / 10 min

*ALL PRICES IN PESOS / LATEST RATES BY THE DATE OF PUBLISHING, WINTER 2022

They have long-term rentals available too. Check out econduce.mx for more info.

📷 ECONDUCE

A WORD ABOUT DRIVING IN MEXICO...

These scooters are a convenient and affordable way of moving around. However, Mexico City is (in)famous for its aggressive driving and drivers. Seriously, all throughout the country, whenever someone's driving fast and aggressively, we say that they're driving like a "chilango" (someone from Mexico City). I strongly suggest only hopping on these scooters if you are pretty experienced in driving a bike. And to never, ever go out into big avenues. Safety first, always.

Bonus...
HOP ON - HOP OFF BUS AKA THE TURIBUS

A red double-decker bus that goes around the city. Before you cringe at how touristy this sounds...hear me out. Mexico City is vast and wide and known for its heavy traffic. These buses are a friendly, safe way to move around the city while you're getting to know it. And If you're on a tight schedule, you get to cover a lot of ground and take a lot in a short amount of time.

The Turibus runs around 4 different circuits, and you can connect between them. Why sit in traffic in an Uber when you can sit on an open bus, take in the view and learn about Mexico City's rich history. Their audio guides are available in 9 different languages and the cost of one ticket is what one Uber ride to the airport usually costs.

⊙ **When:** Daily 9am - 7pm. Buses run every 30 min. by each stop.
♥ **Where:** You can hop on at any stop. Check the closest to you on their webpage.
🏷 **Budget:** $
⊕ Turibus.com.mx

☞ Learn all about the Turibus on page 96.

Tips & Advice

You are not going to be the fumbling tourist. No no no. Because you, my dear, know the cultural norms that will allow you to navigate this foreign land like you've been here before or somethin'.

Here are the Do's and Don'ts of Mexico City...

DO'S

♥ Do Haggle

For all street products (except food), you can haggle. Sarongs, sunglasses, motorbike rentals, even taxi drivers that you find on the street! The first price is rarely the final price. If a lady offers you a shirt for 200 pesos, know that the acceptable price is most likely closer to 125 pesos. Be playful and be reasonable so that everybody wins.

♥ Do Tip Your Salon Lady or Restaurant Server

Tipping isn't always customary in Mexico. But when it comes to beauty services and restaurants, a 10-15% tip is appreciated.

♥ Do Ask For Your Bill

Maybe you want five more beers! The server won't drop your check until you ask for it! When you're ready for your bill, you can say, "La cuenta, por favor".

♥ Do Pack Accordingly

I first came to Mexico City in November, and I didn't pack right. I really didn't believe that Mexico could actually be chilly. Light layers are the key to success. Plus, being such a big, international city - fashion here is hot! The streets are full of stylish people walking around so this is the place to bring all your fun clothes and leopard print.

♥ Do Practice the Safe Code BEFORE Locking the Safe

Before you put your belongings in your room's safe, practice the code. You can reset a safe code with the button inside the safe, near the hinge of the door. Always reset the safe, enter your pin and then practice opening and closing the safe a couple of times before you lock your stuff in there. OH and make sure the safe keys aren't INSIDE the safe.

♥ Do Carry Cash

All restaurants and shops will take cards. But for your local adventures (markets, transportation, shops) you will need cash. You can find ATMs all around town.

♥ Do Avoid Peak Hours at Restaurants

In one of the most populated cities on earth, restaurants are bound to get crowded. Plan ahead and make reservations either through OpenTable or directly with the restaurant. But, if you want to roam freely and not book in advance, the trick is to eat or have dinner at non-peak hours. Luckily, Mexicans eat on a different schedule. Peak hour for lunch is usually around 2 pm, while dinner is around 8pm.

♥ Do Check What Events Are Going On Beforehand

There is always something (well, more like multiple things) going on in Mexico City. Incredible art exhibits, design weeks, festivals, and concerts. Check-in advance so you can plan around it. Jump to our Festivals & Holidays section on page 260 to learn more about festivals and exciting things that happen in Mexico City throughout the year.

♥ Do Be Prepared for Altitude Sickness

For the record, I've never experienced altitude sickness or symptoms in Mexico City. Some people do and some people don't. But. If you feel out of breath from just one flight of stairs, that's normal and it will go away after a couple days. This is because Mexico City has an elevation of 7,350 ft.

PRO TIP! If you experience some symptoms, you can take some ibuprofen or paracetamol, or some anti-sickness medication. And don't forget to drink lots of water.

♥ Do Use Airbnb Experience Tours

Jungle hikes. Surf lessons. Food tours. Even authentic shaman healings. I love to link up with locals excited to show you around their backyard via Airbnb Experiences. Tours are created with love and the profits go directly to those who deserve em'.

Ps. No, I do not get any kind of commission for Airbnb Experiences. I'm just obsessed with exploring new places with locals. But hey, give me some street cred. When you go on an Airbnb Tour, let the hosts know I sent you!

DON'TS

✘ Don't Do Drugs

It's a big city with a big party scene. You will inevitably be offered drugs. Please know that drugs are highly illegal in Mexico and if you're caught and can't pay the bribe, you can expect to sit in a Mexican jail for months before you get a fair trial. Plus, taking drugs could mean putting yourself in a vulnerable position. Stay off drugs, kids. Drink Tequila instead.

✘ Don't Try to Buy Anything Illegal

Drugs. Exotic animals. Babies. Remember that if you go looking for trouble in Mexico, you'll find it. Just be prepared to bribe your way out of a situation if you get caught.

✘ Don't Support Animal Tourism

Dolphin shows. Iguana pictures. If you want to be an ethical traveler, don't give money to people or industries that exploit animals.

✘ Don't Drink the Water

In general, Mexico's tap water is safe to shower in and brush your teeth with, but it's not safe to drink.

✘ Don't Drive a Car

Mexico City traffic is (in)famous for being heavy, hectic, and aggressive. With so many transportation options available, avoid driving a car unless you really, really, really have to.

Safe Girl Tips for Mexico City

A quick briefing…

☞ Violent crime against tourists is rare within the neighborhoods that I guide you to in this book.

☞ Crime here typically comes in the form of pickpockets or phone-snatching rather than actual violence.

☞ Assault is more likely to happen between two travelers, rather than a traveler and a local.

✳ Don't Go to These Neighborhoods…

Every big city has its own not-so-friendly corners that you should stay away from. Just be aware of the names so you don't end up there.

→ Tepito

→ Ciudad

→ Iztapalapa

→ Doctores has a bad reputation but is still safe to wander during the day. It's starting to change and some new things are starting to pop there. Just avoid going there alone at night.

✳ Don't Walk Around with Your Phone Out at Night

Once, I was making an Instagram Story while waiting for my Uber in Centro Historico. It was nighttime. When I got in the car, my driver lectured me (out of love) and told me that I was lucky no one snatched my phone out of my hands. Oops. Don't be waving your phone around at night where someone can swipe it from you.

✳ Wear a Cross Shoulder Bag or Fanny Pack

You don't really have to worry about someone coming over, grabbing your purse off you and running away. But if your bag is hanging loosely by your side, wandering hands can find a way to snatch your stuff (particularly in super crowded areas or public transportation).

Wearing a cross-shoulder bag or a fanny pack is the best way to keep your belongings secure and is an assurance that you won't take your bag off to place it by your feet, on the table, or the chair beside you… because that's another place where it can get swiped, and you won't even notice.

Keep your bag where you can see it and feel it. If you're walking through crowded areas, make sure it's always in front of you. Check my travel store for the best cross-shoulder purses and fanny packs!

✳ Look Both Ways Before You Cross the Street

Duh, but really- traffic here is different than back home. Pedestrians don't have the right of way here- even on a green light. When crossing the street, don't just look for cars. Also, look for motorbikes that whiz between the cars!

✳ Drive Super Carefully

Either a scooter or a motorbike or even a car, if you're going to drive, be extra careful. One false move after two drinks too many, your tire slips in the dust and bam – accident. Even if you think that you're okay after a few drinks, it's the other reckless idiots you've got to watch out for. You need quick reaction times to avoid drunk drivers after sunset – so keep all of your wits about you by driving totally sober.

✳ Walking at Night

Make smart choices. Stay on lit roads, don't walk down a dark alleyway or an empty street late at night. Walk with a friend when possible, and don't get super drunk and wander off by yourself. Follow those common sense rules, and you'll be safe as can be.

✳ Avoid Street Taxis

It's not that street taxis are particularly unsafe, but with so many transportation options that you can track and share, it's always better to stick to that option! Street Taxis in Mexico City are white and pink, so they're easy to recognize.

Safety Bonus!
WHAT DO YOU DO IN CASE OF AN EARTHQUAKE?

By now, you know Mexico City can be prone to earthquakes. And I know it can be a scary thing to talk about, but it's important to be prepared before coming to Mexico City.

First of all, don't panic. Earthquakes aren't a dime a dozen. They can happen, but that doesn't mean there's one every week or every month. It's a rare occurrence. But I feel that very few people know about this before their arrival, and this kind of information can be life-changing. Literally.

☞ Download Skyalert On Your Phone

SkyAlert is a natural disaster warning system that will alert you of an upcoming earthquake. There are radio sensors that detect earthquakes all over the city, and that go off 45-50 seconds before the quake. Giving you a good window to act or evacuate. SkyAlert gives you a 60-second window, 10 more seconds than the alarm.

☞ Know Your Evacuation Routes

If you're staying in a hotel, you'll see several signs with the evacuation routes on the walls. You can always ask the concierge or the people in charge for them, too.

☞ Look for a Safe Spot

If you must remain indoors, look for a safe spot. Get under a table or a desk or against an interior wall. Another sturdy spot is inside any door frame. Avoid exterior walls, windows (and glass in general), heavy furniture, and appliances. Stay clear of the kitchen and avoid elevators.

☞ Stay in the Open

If you're outdoors or you've evacuated, stay in the open, away from powerlines, buildings, or anything that could potentially fall down. If you were driving when the quake happened, pull over and stay away from traffic.

☞ After the quake...

Evacuate the building until you're sure it's safe to reenter. Look for assembly points outside and follow the Civil Protection brigades' instructions. Contact family and friends when possible to let them know you're safe!

But again, don't panic. This is just information to know and have, just in case. My sister and many dear friends have gone through a few earthquakes and earthquake scares, and they've always been safe and sound. And despite this, they still choose to live in this beautiful, vibrant and exciting city.

Things can happen anywhere and anytime, but you and I, we don't let that keep us from exploring the world. We pack our wisdom and get ready to tackle whatever travel throws our way.

- EMILIA

LET'S TALK ABOUT SEXUAL ASSAULT

Foreign women (that's us) are statistically more likely to be sexually assaulted by a foreign man (other travelers) on holiday than they are to be sexually assaulted by a Mexican man. Think about it; in hostels, hotels, and bars - we are more likely to be hanging around foreign men, quite possibly with alcohol in our systems, and therefore exposed to that risk. Just like you would at home, monitor your sobriety levels and be aware of your surroundings.

♥ **BIGGEST SAFE GIRL TIP:**
Don't trust other travelers blindly. Oftentimes, we think we need to protect ourselves from the locals, and so we overlook the possible danger of fully trusting a cute new guy in our hostel or a woman that looks like our sister. The truth is, there are criminals everywhere. More often than not, sexual assault is committed traveler-on-traveler rather than local-on-traveler. So don't get too drunk with those strangers you just met. When meeting new people, trust your gut always!

♥ **MY #1 DATING TIP:**
That guy you want to sleep with? Before you take him home, ask him to take a picture of his ID and send it to your friend. If he had malicious intentions before…he might reconsider his plans now that he can be held accountable. Also, take him to YOUR PLACE the first few nights. Do not go to his place until you feel like you know him.

Remember, Always Prioritize Your Comfort Over Being Polite.

NERVOUS?
Even I get nervous before (and during) a new trip. The secret? Turn that nervous energy into excited energy. Instead of saying "I'm afraid to do this" say "I can't wait to do this" and let life happen.

MEXICO CITY
Airport Guide

Common Name: Aeropuerto Internacional de la Ciudad de Mexico (AICM)
Official Name: Aeropuerto Internacional Benito Juarez de la Ciudad de Mexico (AICM)
Airport Code: MEX
Location: A 25-minute drive to Roma Norte (depending on traffic).
Language: Signs in English and Spanish
Wifi: Free…but not always the strongest.
Open: This is a 24-hour airport with some shopping and restaurants open 24-hours.

But in many places you'll see this airport referred to as "AICM". We will refer to this airport's code as MEX - but if you see AICM on your flight confirmation, now you won't panic.

Mexico City Airport has two terminals (T1 and T2). Terminal 1 is usually the international terminal for landing and departure, however, Terminal 2 is home to most AeroMexico flights.

Always check on which terminal you're arriving / departing from to plan your arrival accordingly.

How to Get Between T1 and T2:
(if you have a connecting flight or go to the wrong terminal)
→ **Free Train:** All train passengers must have a ticket (physical or electronic) or a reservation code and carry-on luggage only. No checked luggage. The train runs from 5:00AM – 11:00PM, and the journey takes less than 5 minutes.
→ **The Bus:** If you have checked luggage, you must use the bus to change terminals. Buses can be found at Entrance 6 of Terminal 1 and Entrance 4 of Terminal 2 and costs $6-$16 pesos (that's cheap).

✈ ARRIVING AT MEX

Most international flights land in Terminal 1. But if you happen to fly with AeroMexico, you might be landing in Terminal 2.

This airport gets busy! While you can expect lots of people when you land, you can also expect lots of help! If ever you get overwhelmed, find an information desk or approach any airport staff for directions. You aren't the first person to need some guidance, although, with this airport guide, you should be prepared!

Here's what to expect as you arrive on either terminal!

❶ STEP ONE: Fill Out The Forms on The Flight.
You'll have customs forms and declaration forms that will ask you basic stuff: who you are, where you're staying, and whether you are bringing things you need to declare, such as $10,000 (no, you're not… right?).

❷ STEP TWO: Head Toward Immigration
The immigration officers will ask you where you're staying and how long you're staying. Have a general plan. You don't have to have a flight out yet, but have an answer ready. They just want to know that you're a) coming on vacation and b) leaving eventually. Don't overcomplicate it.

❸ STEP THREE: Get Your Luggage
After baggage claim, you'll go through customs. You will have a declaration form. And most likely, you have nothing to declare. You'll hand that form to the officers and proceed through, but you may possibly be chosen for a baggage check. This is normal.

❹ STEP FOUR: Arrive!
You're officially in Mexico after you leave baggage claim! Bienvenida!

❺ STEP FIVE: Wifi or Get a Sim Card

There's free Wi-Fi in the Mexico City airport, but it doesn't always fully work. And if you don't have Google Fi to connect to the internet, you'll need a local SIM Card.

SIM Cards are cheap and easy to get in Mexico. The best option is to get a TELCEL SIM Card because they have the most coverage.

Once you land, you can get your Telcel SIM Card in Terminal 1 in the following spots:
- → **Official Telcel Store:** Gate 5, on the 2nd floor
- → **OXXO:** Gates 6 & 7, and also in the lobby
- → **7Eleven:** Gate 8

Ask for a SimCard or for a "chip" for Telcel. They will give you a small card with your local number, and they can help you install it on your phone if you need it. An internet package of $200 pesos will be pretty enough for 1 month. Just say: **"Paquete de Internet de Doscientos pesos"**...or show this phrase to the clerk.

PRO TIP! Make sure your phone is unlocked for other SimCards before departing home.

❻ STEP SIX: Transport to Your Hotel

Option 1: Ride-sharing Apps
The easiest way to do this is by taking an Uber, Didi, or any of the ride-sharing apps we covered in the Transportation section.

How to Get an Uber:
I give you a step-by-step rundown on how to get an Uber when you land in this video…

⚐ Where:
- → **Terminal 1:** Usually the meeting point is the exit of Gate 3 or 4
- → **Terminal 2:** At the exit of Gate 2

An Uber ride to the areas covered in this book is usually between $150 and $250 pesos ($8-5-$15 USD) but...

Option 2: Company Taxis
With such a high demand for ride-sharing apps lately, prices are insane sometimes. Airport Taxi Companies are the next best option since their prices are regulated and are sometimes cheaper than the apps. Ps. They're totally safe!

How to Get a Taxi:
Once you have passed through customs, you have your luggage, and you exit into the airport lobby.

⊙ **Taxi Hours:** Daily, 24 hours
♥ **Where:**
→ **Terminal 1:** Gates 9 and 10 at the Domestic Area, Gate 1 at the International Area
→ **Terminal 2:** Gate 4 at the Domestic Area / Gate 3 at the International Area

Find the yellow signs for **Taxi 300 or YellowCab**. Emy and her family have used these two companies for years.

Company Taxi rates are calculated by distance and vary depending on where you're going but usually, a regular taxi will cost you between $250 and $300 pesos ($12-$15 USD) to head to any of the areas covered in this book.

Here's a list of their current average prices:

ROMA NORTE & SUR	around $250 pesos
CENTRO Historico:	around $250 pesos
COLONIA JUÁREZ:	around $250 pesos
COLONIA Cuauhtemoc:	around $250 pesos
COLONIA CONDESA:	around $270 pesos
SAN MIGUEL CHAPULTEPEC:	around $250 pesos
Coyoacan:	around $300 pesos
POLANCO:	around $300 pesos

TAXI PRO TIP! Make sure you have your hotel or AirBnb's address at hand, so you can show it to the teller and driver.

⚠ **Avoid people who approach you with Taxi signs**, those are tourist traps and will charge you "las perlas de la virgen" (Virgin Mary's pearls - Mexican slang to say that they will rob you blind). A simple "No, gracias" will suffice, and keep on walking.

✈ DEPARTING FROM ACIM

Step 1: Get to The Airport
You can either get an Uber/Didi or a Company Taxi.

You can book a YellowCab Taxi (a trusted and verified Taxi Company) on their website:
→ Visit ⊕ taxisyellowcab.com/reserva.php to book directly.
→ Or you can contact them via Whatsapp: +52 55 2599 6024

You'll need to fill in all of your departure information, and you'll get a confirmation in your email.

The prices are pretty much the same as in the table above.

Step 2: Check-In and chill.
Once at the airport, the rest will be pretty standard for you. No big surprises. The only extra step is to go through customs if you're leaving the country.

But Here are Some Extra Departure Tips:
✳ Leave your hotel towards the airport with plenty of time because you never know with Mexico City traffic! You'd rather be early than late!
✳ Triple-check that you have everything with you, triple-check your flight time, and triple-check your gate once you get to the airport.

✳Need any snacks or an inflatable neck pillow for your flight? Terminal 1 has a lot of restaurants and shops where you can do some last-minute shopping.

✳Do you have a Priority Pass or access to the lounges? Most lounges are located around gate 15; just make sure you have ample time to walk to your gate. This airport is big.

KIND-HEARTED PRO TIP: On the way to the airport, have your left-over pesos in your pocket ready to distribute. You will always have some leftover pesos - and they're no use sitting in a drawer at home! Instead, have them ready to pass out to street performers or hawkers. Give some tips or buy a couple of extra souvenirs. This is a good karma way to end your trip!

✈ **IMPORANT NOTE: There's a new airport in Mexico City but...**
There's a new airport in Mexico City called Felipe Angeles International Airport (abbreviated as AIFA). So far, it only hosts a few national flights and international flights to South America. There's a veeeeery slim chance you'll land or depart from here.

However, few domestic flights do depart from this new airport. If you're planning on doing some travels within the country, I'd recommend that you try to avoid departing or landing at this airport. It's very far away from the city, and it's expensive to get to and from there. But if you must, fear not; just know ahead that you'll need to budget a little bit more for your ride to get to/from this airport.

✒ **How Much:** An average Uber ride to this new airport from Roma / Condesa will cost around $600 pesos ($30 USD).

Congrats! You've completed the Survival Guide!
Now, on to much more fun stuff!

THE
Mexico City
BUCKET LIST

I love to travel with a bucket list instead of an itinerary, so let me start you off with these magical gems to help your itinerary fall together.

To help you start envisioning what your dream trip looks like, you need a Bucket List.

I've created a few bucket lists, actually. These are the things that I recommend you plan your trip around.

Pay attention to the neighborhoods, this will help you decide where you want to stay and how you want to organize your itinerary.

TOP 10 PLACES TO STAY

 01 Nima Local House, Roma Norte

02 Pug Seal Polanco Anatole France, Polanco

 03 La Valise Mexico City, Roma Norte

04 La Palomilla Bed & Breakfast, Between Condesa and Roma Norte

 05 Ryo Kan, Juárez

06 Hostal Regina, Centro Historico

 07 Círculo Mexicano, Centro Historico

08 Agata Hotel Boutique & Spa, Coyoacan

 09 Hotel W Mexico City, Polanco

10 Downtown Mexico, Centro Historico

TOP 10 MEXICAN FOOD SPOTS TO EAT

01 Expendio de Maíz, Roma

02 Molino El Pujol, Condesa

03 Tacos Los Cocuyos, Centro Historico

04 Guzina Oaxaca, Polanco

05 El Cardenal, Centro Historico

06 Taqueria Orinoco, Condesa

07 Tacos Los Parados, Roma

08 Siembra Tortilleria, Polanco

09 Birria Colorado, Roma & Juarez

10 Caldos de Gallina y Enchiladas Luis, Roma

BOUGIE BONUS! Pujol, Polanco…one of Mexico City's top fine dining experiences from star chef Enrique Olvera. Ps. You have to book plenty of time ahead if you want to grab a spot!

TOP 5 SAFEST MARKETS

01 Mercado Coyoacan, Coyoacan

02 Mercado Medellín, Cuauhtemoc

03 Tuesday Tianguis Condesa, Condesa

04 Mercado La Ciudadela, Centro Historico

05 Bazar del Sábado, San Angel

Bonus! Mercado Roma, Roma Norte

TOP 10 DATE SPOTS

01 Loup Bar, Roma Norte

02 Hugo El Wine Bar, Roma Norte

03 Casa Olympia, Polanco

04 Felina, Condesa

05 Rosetta, Roma Norte

06 Ciena, Condesa

07 Sartoria, Roma Norte

08 Maximo Bistrot, Roma Norte

09 Le Tachinomi Desu, Juarez

10 Expendio de Maiz, Roma…for an adventurous food date where you might try insects! My boyfriend and I had a blast here but make sure you read what I write about this restaurant on page 141.

FUN FACT: Emy's sister, Ximena, owns this kinda famous restaurant with her French husband, alongside talented chef Joaquin Cardoso: Loup Bar, Roma Norte

TOP 10 CULTURAL EXPERIENCES

01 Go on a Food Safari with Eat Like A Local MX

02 Ride the Coyoacan Tram

03 See the Teotihuacan Pyramids

04 Listen to some Mariachi at Plaza Garibaldi

05 Stroll down the colonial streets and plaza of Centro Historico at night

06 Eat street tacos while standing up (or leaning on a wall)

07 Eat churros in Coyoacan

08 Walk along Paseo de la Reforma

09 Eat lunch aboard a boat in Xochimilco

10 Attend a Lucha Libre Match…yeah, this is culture - don't let the sparkle masks fool you.

TEOTIHUACAN PYRAMIDS

TOP 10 MUSEUMS

01 The Anthropological Museum, Polanco

02 Palacio de Bellas Artes, Centro Historico

03 Franz Meyer Museum, Centro Historico

04 JUMEX Museum, Polanco

05 Popular Art Museum, Centro Historico

06 La Casa Azul (Frida Kahlo's House), Coyoacan

07 Modern Art Museum, Polanco

08 MUAC (University Museum of Contemporary Art), Coyoacan

09 Anahuacalli Museum, Coyoacan

10 MUNAL (National Art Museum), Centro Historico

FUN FACT! Mexico City has the most museums per square meter in the world.

LOCAL PRO TIP!

We asked our friend Alba, a museum expert who was born in Mexico City, **"If you had to choose ONE museum to visit in Mexico City, which one should you choose?"** She says...

"If this is your first time visiting Mexico City, then definitely the Anthropology Museum. It's the biggest and most important in the city, and it will give you a great context about Mexico and our indigenous communities."

Ps. Alba runs @mdemuseos on Instagram and TikTok, a page completely dedicated to museums, most of them in Mexico City, so through it you can have a glimpse of the city's museums. Yes, the content is mostly in Spanish, but you'll get the gist of what's happening through her photos and reels.

Mexico City

BEAUTY & WELLNES GUIDE

NAILS	🗯 HAIR
**A.MORATA	@amorat.a** Fun, artsy, colorful nails **Where:** Roma Norte **Open:** Daily 8am - 8pm **How to Find it:** Álvaro Obregón 70. This place is a bit hidden but you'll find it at the door on the right of the brick-colored facade that is one business to the right from Quentin Cafe.	**PRETTY BITCHES	@prettybsalon** Cuts, colors, Brazilian blowouts, conditioning treatments **Where:** Roma Norte **Open:** Tues - Fri 11am - 8pm / Sat 10am-8pm / Sun / 10am-4pm www.facebook.com/prettybsalon/
**KIKI NAIL BAR	@kininailbar** Gorgeous, classic nails & you can book online **Where:** Locations in Roma Norte, Condesa, Polanco and Juárez **Open:** Mon - Sat 10am - 8pm Book your appointments at kikinailbar.com/citas	**PAPRIKA HAIR SALON	@paprikadf** Emy's sister and nephew get their haircut here **Where:** Roma Norte **Address:** Colima 159, 3rd floor Book your appointment at paprikahairsalon.com/en/ Ps. This place doesn't make appointments via Instagram!

WAX REVOLUTION

@waxreolution

I asked multiple girlfriends in Mexico City where they got waxed and many said Wax Revolution. This place is the holy grail of waxing. I got my Brazilian done in Polanco, fast and easy!

Where: Locations in Polanco, Juarez and Condesa

Check out their website for promos and to make an appointment: www.waxrevolution.com

THE WAX QUEEN

@thewaxqueencdmx

This was the second most common recommendation! I can't wait to try them next time I'm in the city. If you try The Wax Queen before me, message me and let me know how it went!

Where: Condesa
Book via Whatsapp: 55 4482 2169

AWAY SPA AT THE W HOTEL

Massages average around $75 per hour but afterward you can enjoy sitting in the sweat lodge and relaxing in the whirlpool.

Book on their website: https://www.marriott.com/en-us/hotels/mexwm-w-mexico-city/experiences/

REIKI MASSAGE BY MONSE

Massage mixed with energy healing and balancing through Reiki. Monse speaks just a little English but her energy and enthusiasm bridge the gap. The session lasts about 3 hours. It begins with a short interview to discuss what emotional, mental, and physical blockages you have. Then her work begins

Where: At home or hotel. She will come to you and bring a table. Just confirm with your hotel that it's okay for her to visit.
Contact: Message her on Whatsapp and tell her Alexa sent you - +52 55 2321 1626
Pay in cash: 1500 - 1800 pesos depending on location

Cacao Rituals. Temazcal Ceremonies. Energetic healing massages. Women cleansing rituals. Consultation with your higher self through a medium. All the paths to connect with your spiritual self are held on this beautiful green oasis just outside of Mexico City.

Luis and his angels hold group ceremonies and events privately or open to anyone. Message him on Whatsapp before you come to say, "Hey, let me know if any events pop up during these dates" or "Hi, I need some spiritual healing in the form of XYZ," and he will help you organize it.

Ps. These are the same amazing people that I did my Temazcal ceremony with, and wow.

CONTACT LUIS

Email: tuartesanaexperiencias@gmail.com
Whatsapp: +527773019389

7 Best Things

TO DO IN MEXICO CITY

01. THE HOP-ON, HOP-OFF BUS

So. You've landed in Mexico City and you're eager to explore, but this city is so vast that you don't know where to even begin! Enter the Turibus, Mexico City's Hop-On, Hop-Off Bus. It's a double-decker bus that tours around the city, giving you easy access to all the sights!

…I know what you're thinking, though: this sounds like some tourist shit. I get it but trust me! This bus is the best and easiest way to start your trip. Why sit in traffic in an Uber when you can sit on top of the bus, catching the sun, watching the city and absorbing Mexican culture along the way?

And hey, solo female travelers freaking love this bus tour! Solo female travelers and couples and groups! Really, this is the best thing to happen to the Mexico City travel scene…so keep reading and plan to center one of two days of your itinerary around this.

<u>Here's How It Works:</u>
❶ **Step 1:** Choose which "circuit" you want to explore.

❷ **Step 2:** Find any bus stop in the circuit where you'll begin. Wait for the bus. Get on and begin your adventure!

❸ **Step 3:** Ride the bus, see the sights, enjoy the breeze - and then get off wherever you want. Maybe you have a destination in mind (a museum or a market) or maybe you're keeping it spontaneous. When you're ready, hop off and explore.

❹ **Step 4:** After you've walked around, find the circuit bus stop nearest to you, wait for the next bus, get on and repeat.

You can do this all day. And you can do this more than just one day, as there is more than one circuit to explore! This is the cheapest way to see the city, the lowest effort and the most comfortable.

Interest peaked? Let me tell you more...

THE CIRCUITS...

The Turibus runs around 4 different circuits and you can transfer from one to the other (although you'll need separate tickets for each!). I prefer to do one circuit at a time as they're planned out brilliantly.

✳Historic Center Circuit

This is the tour I recommend most! It runs from Polanco (the bougie neighborhood), passing by the Anthropology Museum and the Bosque de Chapultepec all the way to the heart of the Historical District. Despite its name, it's the most comprehensive tour, covering most of the neighborhoods in this book.

It has 16 stops in total where you can hop on and off depending on what you want to see - but I definitely recommend hopping off at the Anthropology Museum for an hour or so!

🏷 **Budget:** $160 pesos / $8 USD on weekdays, $180 / $9 USD on weekends
⊙ **When:** Daily 9am - 7pm
⊙ **Frequency:** Buses run every 30 minutes by each stop

✳Coyoacan (South) Circuit

My second favorite tour! Really, do two tours while you're here! This is such an easy way to get to and from Coyoacan. This circuit has 10 stops in total, including La Casa Azul (Frida Kahlo's museum), and Coyoacan's Historic Center.

✒ **Budget:** $160 pesos / $8 USD on weekdays, $180 / $9 USD on weekends
⊙ **When:** Daily 9am - 7pm
⊙ **Frequency:** Buses run every 1.5 hours by each stop / every 45 minutes on weekends

✳Polanco Circuit

I wouldn't prioritize this circuit because the first two are way more exciting, but if you have plenty of time in the city and want to explore more grounds comfortably on this bus, you can do the Polanco circuit. It has only 9 stops, including Museo Soumaya and Museo Jumex, and Antara Hall, México City's prettiest mall where you can do great shopping. Again, this is a cheap and comfortable way to see the city.

✒ **Budget:** $160 pesos / $8 USD on weekdays, $180 / $9 USD on weekends
⊙ **When:** Daily 11am - 7pm
⊙ **Frequency:** Buses run every 1.5 hours by each stop / every 45 minutes on weekends

✳Basilica Circuit

Jump on this one if you're staying in the city long term and want to have a very local and culturally-religious immersive experience. This circuit has only 3 stops, the main one being the Basilica de Guadalupe, a church dedicated to the Lady of Guadalupe and a catholic mecca where thousands of devotees pilgrimage to every year. Note: buses here run every 90 minutes, instead of 30.

✒ **Budget:**$160 pesos USD on weekdays, $180 / $9 USD on weekends
⊙ **When:** Daily
⊙ **Frequency:** 10am, 11:30am, 1pm, 2:30pm, 4pm, 5:30pm

Ok, I want to hop on! Where do I start?

You can see the maps for each circuit at Turibus.com.mx/en/cdmx/ routes and choose your starting point. Really, just go to wherever is closest to you. You can hop on at any of the stops of the circuits, but here's a rundown on where to start depending on where you're staying:

→ **Roma:** Cibeles Fountain

→ **Condesa:** Cibeles Fountain

→ **Juárez:** Monument to Independence (Ángel de la Independencia)

→ **Cuauhtemoc:** Monument to Independence (Ángel de la Independencia)

→ **Centro Historico:** Bellas Artes

→ **Polanco:** Julio Verne (in the corner of Julio Verne and Emilio Castelar)

→ **Coyoacan:** Coyoacan Historic Center (at Parque Centenario S/N)

Once at the location search for the banners and/or red umbrellas with the Turibus logo on them, and the staff wearing black vests.

What about tickets?

You can purchase your ticket for the day directly at the stop before you hop on, or directly on the bus. But if you like to plan ahead, you can also get them online beforehand at Turibus.com.mx/en/cdmx/routes.

PRO TIP! You can totally use this bus as your main mode of transportation during the day while you're in the city. It's cheaper than ride sharing apps and there are stops all over the city; plus you always know there's a bus coming in the next 30 minutes. It's slower of course, but as long as you're not in a rush to get somewhere, it's a cheap, safe and friendly way to move around.

To really seal the deal...

3 BIG REASONS TO LOVE THE TURIBUS

01. The audio guides are extensive and comprehensive, and will supply you with tons of fun facts and tidbits that will make you a Mexico City expert by the end of the day.

02. It's pretty cheap. An Uber ride from one neighborhood to the other can cost you up to $150 pesos / $7.5 USD...while this bus costs $160 pesos / $8 USD for the entire day.

03. You feel safe. You aren't walking around lost. You are riding around with a birds eye view from the comfort of your seat, and only going out to explore once you feel ready. Then, you can jump right back on the next bus when you're ready for your next adventure (or just when your feet get tired).

Ps. I've done this bus so many times since I was a kid, and any time I'm with a friend from abroad in Mexico City, I take them on the Turibus and I enjoy it all over again myself. It never gets boring and I always learn something new about the city. - Emilia

✎ **TRAVEL NOTES:**

....

....

....

....

....

....

02. GO ON A FOOD SAFARI WITH EAT LIKE A LOCAL

EAT
LIKE A
LOCAL.

If you do one tour and one tour only in Mexico City, this is 100% the tour you should do.

Story time:
When Emy and I first started writing this guide, we researched for female-led travel businesses in the city. And this brought us to Rocio, the badass local chick behind Eat Like a Local. One phone call with Rocio (even before meeting her) and we were already blown away by how aligned Eat Like a Local was to The Solo Girl's Travel Guide's values.

Rocio invited us to join her and her team on a street food night tour along with her entire staff which is a squad of local food-loving women. And it was one of the best travel experiences of our lives. Not only because we got to taste and try so many delicious things, but because we had found a business that was creating such a positive impact, changing people's lives and their communities and spreading the gospel of responsible tourism. And shit, we saw the city like a local! We tasted the city like a local!

Rocio calls her tours Food Safaris, "Tours for Tour Haters". They are immersive experiences that will take you deep into raw local life in Mexico City while tasting real, authentic food. These aren't just tours, they are a whole anthropological adventure.

Why do we love Rocio and Eat Like a Local so much?
First, it runs with an all-female crew of the coolest girls. The team is like a Foodie version of the Spice Girls, each one of them leading incredible tours with their unique twists. Also, Eat Like a Local has the best wages

in the industry, not only for the staff, but for all the vendors involved in the tours. Rocio only includes vendors who work ethically AND have awesome food.

A percentage from every tour goes into improving the conditions in the market and their vendors. She's making a goddamn difference and you can feel it everywhere you go with her.

Coming solo? This is the best tour for you. You will either have an intimate group of up to 6 people to experience the city with, or it might just be you and your Spice Girl guide (who you will definitely want to be friends with).

NOTE: Eat Like A Local tours are a tad pricier than other food tours out there. However, they are totally worth it. Like literally start saving your pennies and do it. Not only because they are bottomless eating, but because you're sure you're supporting an ethical business and the communities you come in contact with.

If you're going to splurge on something on your Mexico City trip, this is the best thing you do it on! And no, this is not an #ad in any way. We just love this company this much. I literally cried on both tours.

Here are the Food Safaris We Love:

MEXICAN FOOD 101 - MARKETS + STREET FOOD
Their best-selling safari. On this tour you'll visit not only Mercado Jamaica and Mercado La Merced, but also four more neighborhoods in total. You'll taste 25 different things and learn everything you need to know about Mexico City in the process.

✒**Budget:** 115 USD (I swear to you, it's worth every penny).
♥ **Where:** Starting point is La Condesa
☉ **When:** 10am - 2pm

FLOWER MARKET BRUNCH

A mix between street food, flowers and markets. This tour is all about colors and flavors. You'll taste different kinds of tacos, seasonal fruit, and some Pulque and Mezcal.

🏷**Budget:** 115 USD
📍 **Where:** Starting point is La Condesa
🕐 **When:** 12pm - 3pm

STREET FOOD AT NIGHT - OFF-BEAT CRASH COURSE

Because morning food and night food are different and Eat Like A Local is here to show you how. On this tour you'll hop around town trying different tacos and tortas, getting to know the parts of the city that come to life when the sun goes down.

🏷**Budget:** 115 USD
📍 **Where:** Starting point is La Condesa
🕐 **When:** 6pm - 9:30 pm / 6:30 pm - 10pm

Learn more about Eat Like a Local and book your tour at eatlikealocal.com.mx

03. ATTEND A LUCHA LIBRE MATCH

Lucha Libre is Mexico's eccentric version of wrestling and is absolutely worth your time. The contenders are known as "luchadores"! They get dressed up in shiny spandex and bright masks and "fight" each other...but really it's just a huge performance with some dramatic storylines that is entertaining and, at times, pretty damn convincing. When you attend, you must decide, will you cheer on the Técnicos (the good guys) or the Rudos (the bad guys)?

When I went to my first Lucha Libre event in Mexico City, I felt like a true peek into two worlds: The world of lucha libre and the world of what locals do for fun! I loved watching the dads with their sons screaming at the wrestlers while using extreme profanity! To find my match, I searched for a Lucha Libre experience on Airbnb Experiences and went with a guide who was able to explain all the cultural context of the match to me, ringside. Our guide even brought us our own masks to wear! There's beer for decent prices which you can buy during the game.

PRO TIP: Go on a Lucha Libre tour where there are other guests joining. This is a great way to meet new people while doing something weird.

FUN FACT! Lucha Libre was declared intangible cultural heritage in Mexico in 2018. Famous luchadores have become some sort of superheroes, showing up in comics, movies and merch. Mexican pop-culture at its finest.

♥ **Where:** Best option is Arena México in Colonia Doctores
⊙ **When:** Tuesdays at 7:30 pm, Fridays at 8:30 pm and Sundays at 5:00 pm.
⚤**Budget:** Usually $30-$70 USD per person for the airbnb experience which includes a guide and usually food before the match.

Wanna go cheaper? You can try to buy a ticket at the venue...but matches often sell out. If they're available, here's a tip: The closer to ringside, the better. But hey, Colonia Doctores doesn't have the best reputation for safety so don't go alone.

04. VISIT THE TEOTIHUACAN PYRAMIDS

First, let's learn how to pronounce this. Repeat after me: teo-tiwa-kan. Perfect, let's go.

Even though it's quite touristy and everyone's doing it, visiting the pyramids is a must! Teotihuacan is a Unesco World Heritage Site and one of Mexico's most important archaeological sites in all of Mexico. It is an ancient Mesoamerican city, located 25 miles from modern-day Mexico City. It was the largest city in the Americas of the pre-Columbian era. While it's commonly referred to as an Aztec city...this was built between the 1st and 7th Centuries A.D.,, way before the Aztecs reigned the area and claimed by them in the 1400s.

Teotihuacan is famous for its gigantic monuments, especially the Temple of Quetzalcoatl and the Pyramids of the Sun and the Moon, all laid out along the Avenue of the Dead. Today, it preserves its complex urban design, residential areas, monuments, and murals.

NOTE: Before you go all the way there and are disappointed...it is currently not allowed to climb some of the pyramids. Bummer, I know, but still worth the visit!

🖉 **Budget:** $80 pesos
⊙ **Open:**
Archeological site: 9am - 5pm
Museum and exhibits: 9am - 4:30pm
♀ **Where:** San Juan Teotihuacán, about an hour from Mexico City

Best Way to Go: On a tour. There are tours all over Airbnb Experiences that range from half-day trips to all-day trips with extra adventures mixed in. Take your pick, use reviews to decide!

On this trip, the hosts take you to their grandma's house for a homemade Mexican lunch (spoiler: the main course is her 52-ingredient mole which has been a family recipe for generations).

SEE THE PYRAMIDS FROM THE AIR

If you want to hit the pyramids in a less touristy and more epic way, you can do a Hot Air Balloon experience. This is the coolest way to see the pyramids, and really the only way to actually take in the vastness of this archeological site.

 ## OR SEE THE PYRAMIDS WHILE ON A SCAVENGER HUNT

05. EAT AND DRINK ABOARD A TRAJINERA IN XOCHIMILCO

You've probably seen somewhere photos of colorful boats, crowned with flowers and names and wondered what that was all about. That, my love, is a Trajinera (trah-hee-neh-rah), and it's a unique experience you can only live in Xochimilco (so-cheem-meel-koh), in the south of Mexico City.

Let's get some context, shall we? Xochimilco is a network of canals known as The Floating Gardens.

Bright and Insta-friendly gondola-like flat boats where you can cruise the canals as you sample Mexican snacks and drink tequila as you're serenaded by mariachis. A full-blown Mexican postcard that sounds touristy as hell, right? Not really! You'll be surprised to know and see that Xochimilco is always full of locals too: groups of friends and families celebrating special occasions, laughing and drinking in this cultural version of a party boat.

This is an experience I wouldn't recommend doing solo. Join a tour or create your own party of girls by asking other travel girls to join you. Visit our Facebook community called Girls in Mexico City to start making friends.

Tour Options:

This tour is a bit boozy:

 This tour on Get Your Guide includes more must-see sights like visiting Frida Khalo's home!

💰**Budget:** Trajineras are approx. $25 USD / $500 pesos per hour per boat, not per person (the basic tour is around 1 hour) - and you can negotiate the price a bit. Start with $700-$800 ($35-$40 USD) pesos for 2 hours and go from there!

☉ **Open:** Boats start at 9am and end at 6pm

♀ **Where:** Xochimilco

♀ **Time Needed:** 4-5 hours total

↺ **How To Get There DIY:** There are different "embarcaderos" (ports) where you can start your Xochimilco adventure.

→ The Nuevo Nativitas is the best embarcadero to head to.

→ Avoid the Belen de las Flores embarcadero.

SOME PRO TIPS:

→ Keep in mind that a ride to get to the port will cost around $200-$300 pesos from the city center to Xochimilco, which is normal for an hour ride. To head back, you can order an Uber or a Didi to the Nuevo Nativitas Embarcadero, but I'd recommend you leave before 6pm to avoid rush hour and a surge in prices. There will be taxis waiting at the embarcadero too, but stick with ride sharing apps so your ride can be tracked and shared.

→ Oh, and ignore the guys on bikes that will likely approach your Uber or car saying that they will guide you to the embarcaderos, they will just direct you to the tourist traps.

→ If you want to keep costs lower, you can bring your own snacks and drinks to enjoy on your tour.

→ Make sure to have some small coins for the bathrooms at the embarcaderos (ports).

📷 @SRCHARLES

06. TEMAZCAL CEREMONY

I didn't expect to have such a beautifully intense spiritual experience in Mexico City! When I signed up for this Airbnb Experience, what I understood was that I was going to the outskirts of Mexico City to sit in a pitchblack sweat lodge with a shaman who would sing some songs and we would get a little sweaty while witnessing ancient traditions. What I got was so much more.

Some context: a Temazcal Ceremony is an ancient Aztec ritual for warriors. In the dark of the Temazcal Ceremony, you face yourself, your fears and your deepest wishes full on.

And hey, if you don't have spiritual experiences, you'll still get all the juicy health benefits. Temazcal Ceremonies detoxify the body, help with arthritis, cleanse the respiratory system and give your skin a really beautiful glow - to name a few.

Before you go, get hydrated! You're going to sweat. And when you leave, plan to go get tacos immediately after. You'll be hungry.

Nervous or claustrophobic? Sit next to the door of the sweat lodge. They'll open the flap on occasion or when you need it. But aim to push through any fear or resistence you feel. For me, all my hesitancy showed up in the first 10 minutes of my experience. I really didn't want to let go of control, something you need to do while sitting in the dark, but I committed to being strong and eventually felt more loved and protected than I've ever felt.

BIGGEST PRO TIP: I know I just massively hyped this up, but go with no expectations. Just an open mind and heart and see what comes to you. Trust your shaman. And hey, even my not-so-spiritual boyfriend cherished his experience. This is for everyone.

Ps. No, there are no drugs or alcohol involved. Just spirits and ancestors.

E-Mail: tuartesanaexperiencias@gmail.com   **Book Here:**

07. FREE WALKING TOURS

Every major city has free walking tours. Yes, free! What's the catch? No catch, really, just tip your guide at the end. The beauty of a free walking tour is that it's an efficient and fun way to see the city through an expert's eyes, and it's the ideal situation for a solo traveler to meet other travelers. Plus, you can afford it.

✳I like **Strawberry Tours.** These guys really have their shit together. Browse their Mexico City tours - which include La Roma, Coyocan, Centro Hisorico and more.

Check them out here: https://strawberrytours.com/mexico-city

✳I also like **Kactus Tours.** These are tours run by university students. They've got a Chapultepec Forest tour and a free taco tour (you just have to pay for the tacos).

Check them out here: https://kactus.com.mx

What's an appropriate amount to tip? Tip whatever you feel! I've tipped tour guides 200 pesos ($10) and I've also tipped 1000 pesos ($50) depending on the tour, the guide and how much I could afford to honor their work without going broke. Do what you can!

Can't tip a lot? Go leave them a review on Google and TripAdvisor! That is so appreciated, you wouldn't believe it!

The rest of your trip should be planned around food.

6 Best Markets

TO VISIT IN MEXICO CITY

These are markets you can easily visit by yourself!
They are easy to reach and safe to explore.

MERCADO COYOACAN

Coyoacan's central market is a traditional and colorful Mexican market that is easy to navigate. It's packed with produce, colorful piñatas, kitchen supplies, and great local food stalls, especially the famous Coyoacan Tostadas. The best place to get these is a stall called, well, Tostadas Coyoacan. Order the shrimp and avocado tostadas or the chicken mole tostadas. Always pair it with an agua fresca (fresh flavored water). This market is mostly local, as Coyoacan isn't as gentrified as other neighborhoods, but you'll still see a few tourists shopping for some souvenirs.

⊘ **Open:** Daily 8am - 8pm
♥ **Where:** Coyoacan
🏬 **Address:** Ignacio Allende S/N

MERCADO LA CIUDADELA

Welcome to souvenir heaven. La Ciudadela is a market entirely dedicated to arts & crafts from every corner of Mexico. Ceramics from Puebla, textiles from Oaxaca, figurines from Nayarit, you can find everything and anything in this tour of colors and textures. Don't forget to bring cash, and yes, it's acceptable to barter a little!

⊘ **Open:** Mon-Sat 10am-7pm / Sun 10am-6pm
♥ **Where:** Centro Historico
🏬 **Address:** Balderas S/N

MERCADO MEDELLÍN

Best for exploring beyond an authentic Mexican market: Mercado Medellin has food, products, and produce from all over Latin America. This market has over 500 stalls selling groceries, spices, salsas, flowers, and more things that make for excellent souvenirs. And, of course, a myriad of food stalls with yummy chilaquiles, tacos, tamales, and all the Mexican goodies you can dream of. Plan to have breakfast or lunch here. Language Tip! "Puesto" means "stall".

⊙ **Open:** Daily 9am - 5pm
♥ Where: Cuauhtemoc
Address: Campeche 101

TUESDAY TIANGUIS CONDESA

A tianguis is a non-permanent market. This particular one pops up every Tuesday in La Condesa, extending over several blocks with various produce, proteins, groceries, and cheese. Oh, the cheese. It's worth coming here just to sample and shop for some traditional queso Oaxaca (Mexican string cheese), and to a food-stall-hop trying different kinds of Mexican snacks. This tianguis is fairly local and never too crowded, so it's not as overwhelming as other markets can be.

⊙ **Open:** Tuesdays 10am - 5pm
♥ Where: Condesa
Address: Pachuca 13

BAZAR DEL SÁBADO

Every Saturday, a group of artisans display and sell their work inside a beautiful old colonial house. Shoes, ceramics, jewelry, a whole trip around the arts & crafts world in just one morning. This market is located in the quaint neighborhood of San Angel, and it's surrounded by cobblestone streets full of art shops and local restaurants that you can explore after hitting the Bazar.

○ **Open:** Saturdays 10am - 7pm
♥ **Where:** San Angel
🏠 **Address:** Plaza San Jacinto 11

MERCADO SAN JUAN

One of Mexico City's oldest and most interesting markets! Come here for an immersion into the most exotic corners of Mexican food. Deer, pheasant, squibs, alligator, iguana, rabbit, scorpions, and spiders are all available here for you to buy or try. I know, I know, this sounds like a sketchy culinary black market, but it actually looks like a slightly more sophisticated version of a traditional Mexican market. Besides the exotic bites, there are also more "normal" stalls selling many imported products and delicacies.

○ **Open:** 7am - 6pm
♥ **Where:** Centro Historico
🏠 **Address:** 2° Calle de Ernesto Pugibet 21

OTHER COOL MARKETS
These markets require street smarts and a local guide.

The following markets aren't in any of the areas we dive into in this book...and they are in areas that aren't too commonly visited by tourists, which can be a safety hazard. You either risk getting lost or you risk looking like an easy target. You just need to go with a local.

I visited these markets with Rocio from EatLikeaLocalMX and wow. She is an expert in these areas and the vendors all know her - so you're not going to get lost and you're less likely to have anyone mess with you.

MERCADO JAMAICA

There's markets for food, there's markets for crafts and then there's Mercado Jamaica. This market is fully dedicated to flowers and it's an entire voyage through a sea of colors. You can find native and national flora but entire cold rooms filled with freshly-arrived Tulips too. Come just to watch and marvel at all the different flowers, or you can get a bouquet to brighten your hotel room during your stay. If you come around Day of the Dead, this place turns into a bright yellow stream of Marigold being purchased to prepare the altars.

⊙ **Open:** Daily 12pm - 12am
♥ **Where:** Tláhuac
🛕 **Address:** Guillermo Prieto 45

MERCADO SONORA

Welcome to the Twilight Zone…or at least the Mexican version of it. Mercado Sonora is all about the esoteric: serpentine halls and stalls stacked with crystals, incense, tarot decks, and tarot readers, witchy ingredients for spells, and herbology remedies for any ailment you can imagine. But also to shamanism and darker things like Voodoo and the Santa Muerte (a Mexican religion devoted to death). This is Mexican Mysticism at its finest, a bit macabre for sure, but interesting as hell to visit.

⊙ **Open:** Mon - Sat 8am - 6pm / Sun 8am - 4pm
♥ **Where:** Merced Balbuena
🛕 **Address:** Fray Servando Teresa de Mier 419

MERCADO LA MERCED

This is the largest market in Mexico City and it's been one of the main markets since the 1600's. La Merced is an endless maze of bustling stalls selling food, produce, spices, crickets, crafts, candy, and everything under the Mexican market scope. Needless to say, this place can be overwhelming, so it's best to visit in the hands of experts. Our friends from Eat Like a Local have a tour that includes this market, where you'll be guided by Wendy, Montse and Arely, a family of local girls who were born and raised in this very market…and who will teach you how to make a mean michelada. Book your tour at EatLikeALocal.mx

⊙ **Open:** Daily 8am - 6pm
♀ **Where:** Merced Balbuena
🚕 **Address:** Circunvalación S/N

BONUS! LA LAGUNILLA

This is a bonus because this almost counts as a day trip…and something you should do if you're staying longer in the city.. This flea market is a goldmine for finding antiques: awesome vintage clothes, old records, pieces of furniture, jewelry, you name it. Seriously, Emy's sister is a huge fan of La Lagunilla and has beautiful decor pieces in her Mexico City home that she's scored here. La Lagunilla is a full-morning adventure where you'll find from crazy cheap knick-knacks to other a-bit-more-expensive treasures, but even if you don't buy anything, it can be such a fun thing to do. Get yourself a michelada, browse and haggle away!

⊙ **Open:** Sundays 9am - 3pm
♀ **Where:** Start at the Boxeador Monument Park on Avenida Reforma
🚕 **Address:** Eje 1 Norte (Rayón)

Ps. Eat Like A Local also has a Lagunilla Tour.

LOCAL PRO TIP!
If you had to choose only one market to visit, which one would it be?

"Bazar del Sábado! Because it's fun and colorful and it's very, very Mexican..." - Pablo, Emy's 10-year-old nephew who has grown up in the city and is a little Mexico City connoisseur. And you know what they say, kids always tell the truth!

Where to Stay

IN MEXICO CITY

Where you stay will make or break your trip! That is why I am putting your hotel section front and center.

I'm going to give you all your hotel options right here, organized by area.

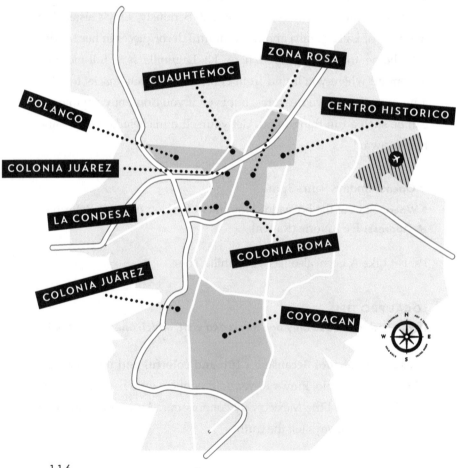

I recommend that you stay in at least two neighborhoods while you're here. For example:

→ 2 nights Polanco, 3 nights Roma Sur
→ 4 nights Roma Norte, 3 nights Centro Historico
→ 5 nights Roma Sur, 3 nights Coyocan
→ 2 weeks in Roma Sur, 1 week in Centro Historico

You're going to be moving all around the city during your stay, and breaking up where you're staying means two things:

1. You get to immerse yourself in two neighborhoods
2. You get to create a smooth itinerary that doesn't have you sitting in traffic, crossing the city every damn day

Only have two or three nights in total? You'll be just fine staying in just one neighborhood in this case.

And hey, you don't need to pick a hotel until after you've read this whole book - but maybe highlight the ones that stand out to you and fit your budget. You can circle back later.

COLONIA ROMA

NIMA LOCAL HOUSE HOTEL

I almost don't want to write about Nima Local House Hotel as I'm tempted to keep it my little secret. This is one of the most beautiful boutique hotels in the city. A 1913 historic home with big windows and elegant rooms, - you'll love the warm rays of sunlight waking you up in the morning, having breakfast on the lush rooftop terrace, and the turndown service with little cookies on your pillow in the evening. And the location is unbeatable, with the best bars and restaurants just within walking distance, but without all the noise!

🏷 **Budget:** $$$
📍 **Address:** Colima 236　　　　　⊕ **Book Here:**

BRICK HOTEL

This is a high-end property with high-end design and a high-end spa! Yes, facials, massages, and treatments. It's tucked away behind lush gardens. Staying here is an intimate experience with just ten-rooms, outdoor dining spaces, and a restaurant which makes your odds of bumping into sophisticated world travelers much much more likely than staying at a big ol' hotel with no character.

A little trivia for you: Brick Hotel gets its name from the bricks which were shipped over from England in the early 20th century, used to build a private estate for the original manager of the Bank of London and Mexico. #fancy

Budget: $$$$
Address: Orizaba 95   Book Here:

LA VALISE MEXICO CITY

Often ranked and rated as one of the top hotels in Mexico City! Imagine coming home from your adventure in the big city to someone ready to take care of your every need. There's no better feeling than that. At La Valise Mexico City, that's exactly what you'll get. A small boutique (only 3 rooms) with staff ready to help you plan, problem solve and get around the city. Staying here is an intimate and personal experience, absolutely ideal for solo travelers who want a high-end experience.

Budget: $$$
Address: Tonalá 53   Book Here:

HOTEL MX ROMA

Remote workers and digital nomads, this one's for you. Hotel MX Roma is the kind of place where you'd feel comfortable crashing for a week. You've got every amenity you need: a workspace in your room and on the rooftop, fast wifi, a breakfast buffet, a gym, social spaces, private spaces, staff that is available 24/7, and even bikes that you can take around the city. They've thought of everything.

Budget: $$
Address: Merida 81   Book Here:

EUROSTARS ZONA ROSA SUITES

This is one of my top picks for where to stay when you are spending modestly but still want to sleep in a clean, quiet, private room. This hotel lacks modern ambiance, but damn it's spacious! Your room comes with a living room and a bathtub! It's clean, the staff are fabulous, and it's in a great location! Check out the walking street that comes alive at night, just a couple blocks behind the hotel. In short, if you're coming to explore the city more than you're coming to chill in your room, go with Eurostars.

Ps. The breakfast isn't that exciting. I chose to go find street tacos and hit up local coffee shops instead of wasting precious stomach space here.

Pss. This hotel could be included in Colonia Juarez (Zona Rosa) because it's technically in that neighborhood, but it's so on the border of La Roma, that I use it as my homebase to explore La Roma.

Budget: $$
🛏 **Address:** Londres 115 (near Zona Rosa)   ⊕ **Book Here:**

LA PALOMILLA BED & BREAKFAST

For the foodie! La Palomilla Bed & Breakfast is surrounded by some of the best restaurants and cafes in the city! This is the place to stay if you've come to eat, starting with breakfast. Absolutely book your reservation with the full breakfast. The owner of La Palomilla is a breakfast lover and so, this B&B offers a breakfast menu with amazing traditional dishes perfect to fill your belly before a big day of exploring. La Palomilla also makes freshly baked cookies and offers aguas frescas every afternoon. Told ya! This is foodie heaven.

🖋 **Budget:** $$$
🛏 **Address:** Segunda Cerrada de Guadalajara 10 ⊕ **Book Here:**

LA CONDESA

CASA MANNACH

Introducing this apartment-style accommodation for the girl who plans to work and cook while she's in Mexico City. Sometimes you just want to feel at home and fill your fridge with local goodies. I get it. You've got a few different style and sized apartments to choose from - all of which have access to a shared rooftop terrace and shared kitchen. Not in the cooking mood? There are restaurants and bars right below you! Now you're really feeling like a local.

Budget: $$$
Address: 190 Avenida Mexico   **Book Here:**

CASI BIS

Hello, black out curtains. If good, deep nights' sleep is what you live for, you're going to love the tranquil atmosphere Casa Bis provides after a big day in the city. You've even got insulated windows to keep the noise of the streets out and just in case, there are ear plugs provided. The beds are not too soft, not too hard, and the pillows are just right. There's even overnight security to guard you while you're snoozing! After you wake up from your slumber, hot coffee will be waiting, along with everything that La Condesa has to offer, right outside your doorstep (including the taco spot next door that you have to try)

Budget:: $$
Address: 382 Campeche   **Book Here:**

AYENDA CASA GUBIDXA

Not a backpacker's hostel, but not a fancy hotel either – Ayenda Casa Gubidxa is idyllic for the solo traveling girl who wants her space but also the opportunity to chat with other travelers. This hotel is actually a big apartment-style house with a shared kitchen and balcony where you're bound to run into other travelers if you hang out there for a while. I love that Ayenda Casa has a touch of style with brightly colored walls and thoughtful decor! And all of this for pretty damn cheap!

Budget: $$
Address: 6 Jojutla   **Book Here:**

CASA PANCHA

If I had a little sister who was on a budget but looking to explore the boho areas of the city where she could sip coffees under big trees and blend in with the trendy locals - all without breaking her bank - this is where I'd tell her to stay. In this chic, boho hostel that screams female friendly. You've never seen a hostel cleaner than this in your life. Plus, you can choose to sleep in cozy capsule bunk beds and they have female-only dorms! Be prepared for digital nomads on laptops and other solo female travelers looking for strolling buddies.

💸 **Budget:** $

🏨 **Address:** 90 Avenida Mazatlan   ⊕ **Book Here:**

CENTRO HISTORICO

SELINA

Traveling with your laptop and want to get some work done? Looking to make friends? When you come to Selina, you don't have to worry about finding a place to work or a place to socialize - both elements are built in. Selina is a poshtel-style hostel and hotel chain that is made to facilitate social travel for remote workers.

You'll find office spaces, pool tables, bean bag chairs, TV rooms, a disco with live music, and even morning group yoga - Selina makes it easy for even the shyest of solo travelers to wind up with a crew. Best of all, travelers of all ages stay here! You can choose to stay in a private room or the dorms - take your pick.

💸 **Budget:** $

🏨 **Address:** Izazaga 8 Colonia Centro   ⊕ **Book Here:**

DOWNTOWN MEXICO

Wanna get tipsy in the pool? If you're coming during the warmest months, May to August, treat yourself to Downtown Mexico. They've got a rooftop pool with a lounge area and a bar that will serve you drinks in your bathing suit while you enjoy the spectacular views of the city. Equally important as the pool, the architecture and design of this hotel is like something out of a magazine, especially if you splurge for the Master Suite. And you never have to leave because one of the best restaurants in the area, Azul Historico, is located on the hotel's central patio. This hotel is the total package.

💸 **Budget:** $$$
🏨 **Address:** Isabel la Catolica 30   🌐 **Book Here:**

CÍRCULO MEXICANO

Instagram heaven. The muted decor, the bright blue pool, the views of the cathedral - this place is just begging to be photographed. Not surprising when you learn that this hotel used to be the residence of and was designed by the famous photographer Manuel Alvarez Bravo. Círculo Mexicano ranks as one of my top 10 hotels in the city for the service, the atmosphere, the location near Zocalo Plaza, and the attention to detail, which all just makes you feel like a rich bitch.

💸 **Budget:** $$$
🏨 **Address:** 20 República de Guatemala   🌐 **Book Here:**

UMBRAL HOTEL

Solo ladies who want to meet some travel friends or travel hotties – the rooftop bar and lounge at Umbral Hotel makes that easy to arrange! The scattered lounge chairs, full-on restaurant with an open-seating plan, and dipping pool create a naturally social atmosphere! There's also another bar on site with stools to pull up and chat with the bartender while waiting for a stranger to sit next to you. Part of the Hilton Collection, Umbral has nailed the chic, sexy hotel vibe!

💸 **Budget:** $$$
🏨 **Address:** Calle de Venustiano Carranza 69   🌐 **Book Here:**

HOSTAL REGINA

Looking for the party hostel? You've finally found it. Don't come to Hostal Regina if you want to keep to yourself. It ain't gonna happen. Hostal Regina is the place for making friends who want to go explore the bars and nightclubs of Mexico City! And it all starts with a pre-party at Hostal Regina's bar. In the morning, the whole hostel commiserates at breakfast where your hangover is cured with juice and carbs! And by the way, the staff here are the best hostel staff in the whole city.

Budget: $

Address: Regina 58 Esquina 5 de Febrero 53 ⊕ **Book Here:**

COLONIA JUAREZ

FOUR SEASONS HOTEL MEXICO CITY

Until you've stayed at a Four Seasons, you'll never understand how a hotel can transform your life. Get ready to be treated like a celebrity with private drivers who pick you up from the airport. With staff who know your name and bring you little treats throughout the day. With gifts and extra special treatment on your days of celebration. If you haven't yet stayed at a Four Seasons, Mexico City Four Seasons is one of the most affordable in the world…but you'll still be treated as if you spent a fortune staying here. Take advantage.

Budget: $$$$

Address: Av. Paseo de la Reforma 500 ⊕ **Book Here:**

RYO KAN

One of the most unique, posh hotel experiences you will ever have can be described in 3 simple words: Rooftop Soaking Tubs. "Ryokan" is actually the Japanese word for a traditional Japanese Inn which features communal bath spaces, which has inspired this concept in Mexico City!

However awkward this may sound, I promise you'll be delighted by the experience of the baths, the architecture, the calm social atmosphere and your extremely comfortable nights' sleep. This is a once-in-a-lifetime hotel experience, my babe.

Budget: $$$

Address: Rio Panuco Numero 166 ⊕ **Book Here:**

CASA PRIM HOTEL BOUTIQUE

Just perfect for a solo girl. Go for the Master Suite with Bath or the Master Suite with Balcony. These two rooms, in any other neighborhood, would cost twice as much! Speaking of neighborhoods, I like the exact location of Casa Prim if you plan to check out both Roma and Centro Historico. You could walk or bike to both. The hotel is chic and trendy and they've got a great rooftop restaurant & bar. Pro tip: Ask for a room that is away from the stairs so you escape the noise.

Budget: $$$
Address: General Prim No. 72   ⊕ **Book Here:**

THE LOCAL WAY - JUAREZ

Just in case you're traveling with friends, I'm going to put this here. It's a 3-bedroom apartment with 4 beds, that when cost is split, works out to be a screaming deal. There's a private living room and kitchen, plus a shared gym and a shared lounging terrace. It's also a short walk to the embassies if you're coming to CDMX for visa-related anything!

Budget: $$
Address: 9 Berlín   ⊕ **Book Here:**

CAPSULE HOSTEL

We're getting more affordable now! When you want to meet fellow travelers but still have some alone time at the end of the day, this is where you come. Instead of open-concept dorm beds, you get a cozy little pod where you sleep without having to stare at anyone next to you. Gone are the days of shaky bunk beds, and here are the days of private reading lights, electric plugs, and privacy curtains! Ps. Capsule Hotel is in a quiet area but just two blocks from the party spots!

Budget: $
Address: Hamburgo 41 Juarez   ⊕ **Book Here:**

HOSTAL JUAREZ

I only discovered this place a couple of weeks after their opening when some friends who where staying there insisted I check it out because it would be "perfect" for this guide. And they were so right! Hostal

Juarez is an artsy hostel located in a former art gallery, created with digital nomads in mind. The rooftop terrace serves as a co-working space by day, and as a social playground by night where they host get-togethers and even art exhibitions on the weekends. If you're a social butterfly looking for a place to make friends, this place is perfect for you. Javier, the owner, is always around and always ready to help you book tours and give you recommendations for the city.

💸 **Budget:** $
🏨 **Address:** Liverpool 28, Colonia Juarez   ⊕ **Book Here:**

CASA EMILIA

If Game of Thrones had a hotel - this is what it would look like. Dim lighting, jewel toned velvet couches, fur blankets, industrial furniture and a castle across the street. It's rough glamor and I want to live here forever. Plus they offer a gorgeous full breakfast for free. If you ever manage to leave, you're located just a quick walk to Chapultepec Park with tons of restaurants and shopping along the way.

💸 **Budget:** $$$
🏨 **Address:** Río Ebro 51   ⊕ **Book Here:**

POLANCO

PUG SEAL POLANCO ANATOLE FRANCE

I stayed in the Presidential Suite with the jacuzzi on the balcony and it was pure bliss. To come home after a long day and soak my feet in the tub while drinking a glass of wine was one of the moments where you think, "This is what life should be". I cannot speak more highly of this hotel, from the whimsical decor to the lounge with free coffee and snacks all day long - I will continue to come back here time and time again.

💸 **Budget:** $$$$
🏨 **Address:** Anatole France 307   ⊕ **Book Here:**

PUG SEAL ALLAN POE

If Pug Seal Anatole France is booked - which it may be as a small boutique hotel - I also love Pug Seal Allan Poe, partially because they put out free tequila every afternoon and partially because their homemade breakfasts are a culinary experience! This line of hotels really nails the guest experience by making you feel like a VIP. You can't go wrong staying here.

🏷 **Budget:** $$$$
🏠 **Address:** Edgar Allan Poe 90   🌐 **Book Here:**

COYOACAN

AGATA HOTEL BOUTIQUE & SPA

I came all the way down to Agata from Polanco. I crossed the city just to come to the spa inside this popular boutique hotel and it was so worth it...but the moment I arrived, I wished I had stayed here! From Agata Hotel, you can walk to the Frida Kahlo Museum and Museo Nacional de Culturas Populares. Even better, you're just a 15-minute Uber away from Mercado Coyocan, which is my favorite market in the city.

🏷 **Budget:** $$
🏠 **Address:** Avenida México 21   🌐 **Book Here:**

H21 HOSPEDAJE BOUTIQUE

You're going to feel pampered here with first class service from the moment you arrive. The hosts watch over you like you are their favorite family members visiting from out of town. They want you to see the best things, eat the best food and feel ultra comfortable when you return home after a day of exploring. They'll help you organize your itinerary and even give you their Whatsapp contact in case you need help while you're out and about. Oh, and if you can, get the room with the balcony!

🏷 **Budget:** $$
🏠 **Address:** 21 Higuera   🌐 **Book Here:**

LA CASITA DE COYOACAN

Budget travelers who are looking for a homey vibe in a safe neighborhood where you can just relax - this is for you! Enjoy breakfast where you can chat with other travelers and perhaps make a few exploring buddies! After your adventures, stop by the 7-Eleven downstairs and grab a couple beers to take to the terrace. This place is laidback.

💵 **Budget:** $$
🏠 **Address:** 14 Tlatetilpa Barrio San Lucas   ⊕ **Book Here:**

Okay baby cakes. Let's learn the neighborhoods!
Get your highlighter ready again!

• •

Now that you have an idea of how this city works, let's take a moment to **set your intention for your trip to Mexico City.** Your intention can be just to have fun and explore, or to spend some quality time with yourself. Maybe your intention is to heal. Or to step outside of your confort zone.

Whatever intention you set, it will set the tone of your trip and call out to the right people and situations aligned with it. Big magic will unfold, you'll see.

✎ **MY INTENTION FOR THIS TRIP TO MEXICO CITY IS...**

....

....

....

....

....

And now....let's discover Mexico City! ♥

CHAPTER ONE

Colonia Roma

THE VIBE:

Safe, walkable, trendy neighborhood with big trees and
infinite options of things to do, see and eat.

BEST FOR:

Eating and drinking at the city's hottest spots

DAYS NEEDED:

At least 2-3 days

Colonia Roma

AKA, "LA ROMA"

If you're new to Mexico City, this neighborhood and the next (La Condesa) are the best areas to start your big city adventure. Let's dive in.

You know how people say NYC is the center of the Universe? Well, Mexico City is the Latin version of NYC, and La Roma is the epicenter of Mexico City.

Roma was one of the first "upper class" neighborhoods in the early 1990s, where Art Nouveau and Art Deco mansions started to pop up as people fled the crowded city center. Until the 1940s, it remained a hub for aristocratic European families, but as the city grew, the area gave into modernization and commerce - and the neighborhood declined. It wasn't until the early 2000s when La Roma began a process of revival which transformed it into the hot spot that it is today.

Mexico City has become a foodie destination, and while the gastronomic movement started in the bougie neighborhood of Polanco, it was here where it was solidified and where it gained the momentum that turned the city into such a sought-after destination. However, La Roma is much more than eating your heart out. Shops, libraries, galleries, museums, indie cinemas...this fashionable district has it all.

Today, "La Roma" is divided into two colonias: "Roma Norte" and "Roma Sur", divided by Alvaro Obregón Avenue:

→ **Roma Norte** is the more notorious half. It's where most of the trendy scene is located. And where most of the insta-worthy colonial buildings and leafy sidewalks are too. The "prettier" side of La Roma, you could say.
→ **Roma Sur** remains more of a "working-class" area. It's in this southern half where you'll have more of a local, authentic Mexican experience.

LA ROMITA

Within La Roma, there's a smaller neighborhood called La Romita. The name translates as "The little Roma". So why the dramatics of having a neighborhood within a neighborhood? Let me explain.

Back when the Spanish conquered the City, this little area was one of the few zones where the Aztecs were allowed to continue to live. And through the years, it developed as an independent neighborhood despite its location. Even when La Roma was occupied by mostly European families, La Romita's residents fought the development and remained socially distinct from the rest of the neighborhood as they were "lower class". Due to this "lower class" status, La Romita gained a gritty reputation.

Fast forward to today, that sour reputation is long gone. La Romita is now considered an easy-breezy oasis to explore away from the buzzing scene in La Roma. Unlike its surrounding neighbor, La Romita still retains a village-like aura. The narrow streets are plastered with street art, and people still greet each other. You won't find trendy cafes but local food joints instead.

Areas to Know in Colonia Roma

ROMA NORTE

Streets are lined with trees, trendy cafes, bars, restaurants, shops, and galleries. You'll recognize this area right away because of the beautiful old mansions and all the greenery around.

ROMA SUR

Cross Coahuila Avenue towards the south, and you'll be in Roma Sur, the more local half of the neighborhood. You'll notice this area has more modern architecture and fewer trees.

LA ROMITA

A little neighborhood inside this neighborhood buried within the streets of Puebla, Durango, and Morelia. A web of narrow alleyways with walls covered in murals full of local places. You'll notice the change of scenery once you step into this village-like urban bubble.

AVENIDA COAHUILA

This avenue serves as the line that divides Roma Norte and Roma Sur.

AVENIDA ALVARO OBREGON

Pretty much La Roma's main avenue and a coveted location for restaurants.

CIBELES FOUNTAIN

A round-about called "Fuente de la Cibeles". Why is this important? Because it's a great point of reference to find yourself, to order a car to and from. Plus, you can find one of the Turibus stops here.

PLAZA RÍO DE JANEIRO

A square/splash park that's an important distinctive feature of Roma Norte. It's at the epicenter of where the trendiest cafes and restaurants are and a nice place to take a stroll. There's a copy of MichelAngelo's David sculpture in the center fountain, so you'll recognize it right away.

PRO TIP! The oscar-nominated movie "Roma" depicts life in this neighborhood in the 1970s, years before it became such a trendy spot. Even though the film is in black and white, it still conveys the spirit and essence of La Roma. The movie is an autobiographical piece by Mexican director Alfonso Cuarón (10-time Oscar-nominee and director of Gravity), and it was shot in Roma Sur, right across from his childhood home. Watch it as you get ready for your trip.

 HEY! I DON'T WANT YOU TO GET LOST. SCAN THIS CODE TO GER YOUR MEXICO CITY MAP!

Where to Eat in Colonia Roma

Brace yourself, this upcoming food section is the biggest food section in any of my guides. Because one of the main things to do in La Roma is eating and drinking. Get ready for a gastronomic adventure.

COFFEE & COWORKING

BUNA

The first coffee shop that Emy insisted on showing me in Mexico city was this snug little spot. Often regarded as one of the finest coffee spots in the city, Buna serves 100% Mexican beans! Besides coffee, they have pastries from Abarrotes Delirio (see the Lunch and Dinner section) on the menu. You'll often see locals here with their laptops as it's one of those places that's easy to relax and focus! **PRO TIP:** Order a latte or a cappuccino with Macadamia Milk at Buna!

⊙ **Open:**8am - 7pm
♥ **Where:** Roma Norte
🛱 **Address:** Orizaba

Ps. They also have another location in La Laguna, in Colonia Doctores. @bunacafemx

CAFE TRUCHA

With new places popping up all the time in Mexico City, it's always hard to pick a favorite, but Cafe Trucha captured my heart at first sip when I tried their Maple Latte. Their menu serves "picnic tapas", the loveliest name for small appetizers if you ask me, and delicious pastries on a little rustic terrace a few steps away from Parque Rio de Janeiro. It's the perfect place to spend some time with your book or journal, but just so you know, the morning can get busy. So either come early or come at the in-between hours.

⊙ **Open:**Mon - Fri 8am - 11pm / Sat 9am - 11pm / Sun 9am - 6pm
♥ **Where:** Steps away from Parque Rio de Janeiro
🛱 **Address:**Plaza Rio de Janeiro 53 Local-2 / @ cafetrucha

CAFE BARAJAS

The best Dirty Chai in the city! I order a Dirty Chai everywhere I go, and this was perfectly foamy and creamy with the perfect balance of sweetness to balance out the chai. The cafe is tiny, so you'll likely sit outside on the street watching life go by. I loved that most of the patrons seemed like daily locals coming to their routine coffee spot. This charm made Cafe Barajas my most memorable cafe experience in Mexico City.

⊙ **Open:** Mon - Sat 12pm - 8pm / Sun 12pm - 6pm
♥ **Where:** Roma Norte
🛏 **Address:** Monterrey 225
@cafe_barajas

CAFEBRERIA EL PENDULO

Remember that scene in Beauty & The Beast where the Beast shows Belle the castle library? This place feels a teensy bit like that. Cafebreria is a made-up word from the words "cafeteria" (coffee shop) and "librería" (book store). Three stories of just books, books, and books. And great coffee. It's a nice little escape for some downtime to read a book and sip a latte. This place is an icon in the city and they have a few locations, but this is my personal favorite.

⊙ **Open:** Mon - Sat 8am - 11pm / Sunday 9am - 10pm
♥ **Where:** Roma Norte
🛏 **Address:** Alvaro Obregon 86
@cafebreriaelpendulo

TIERRA GARAT

This is Mexican Starbucks, basically. Tierra Garat is a beautifully designed coffee shop chain that I often use as a coworking space while sipping ethically sourced Mexican coffee. If you can forgo the caffeine fix, I recommend trying the "chocolate caliente" aka hot chocolate. This isn't the hot chocolate you knew as a kid! You can order your hot chocolate mixed with vanilla, chili, orange, or ginger, amongst other fun variations. And if you need caffeine, just get a side shot of espresso.

⊙ **Open:** Mon - Fri 7am - 10pm / Sat - Sun 8am - 10pm
♥ **Where:** Roma Norte
🛏 **Address:** Durango 353
@tierragarat

ROMPEOLAS CAFE

A tiny café with the best cold brew around. This is where a very niche subsect of locals goes. They also have carajillos, an alcoholic coffee drink that Emilia is obsessed with.

And with good reason, Carajillos are sweet and strong; made with Licor 43 and an espresso shot, they are the perfect middle ground between coffee and dessert. They are usually drunk after a big meal when the post-eating snooze hits, but hey, you're on vacation; there's no wrong time for some boozy coffee.

🕐 **Open:** Mon - Sun 8am - 7:30pm
📍 **Where:** Roma Norte
🍴 **Address:** Chihuahua 142-F
@rompeolascafe

....

CARDINAL CASA DE CAFE

This coffee shop feels less trendy and cozier, full of wooden crates and old globes, quirky details, and colorful cups. They serve specialty beans from micro-productions and local producers, so the coffee they have available is constantly changing. Whatever you're sipping here is guaranteed to be unique but still hits the spot. Cardinal is the perfect spot for some quiet time with a book and a pastry, just like "en casa" (at home).

🕐 **Open:** Mon-Sun 8am-9pm
📍 **Where:** Roma Norte
🍴 **Address:** Cordoba 132
@casacardinal

BREAKFAST & BRUNCH

TACOS ON THE CORNER

No, this isn't the name of a restaurant. I literally mean, if you see a taco stand on the corner with locals lined up in the morning, go there. It's your lucky day! Tacos are breakfast food.

While you'll see some locals heading to a cafe or coffee shop for breakfast, you'll also see many lining up at a taco stand or grabbing a quick pre-wrapped taco from an old man on a corner selling them out of his cooler. There's no right way to do breakfast in Mexico City...but tacos for breakfast can't be wrong.

....

PANADERÍA ROSETTA

This bakery is Rosetta restaurant's little sister (you'll read about them later) and Roma's official pastry heaven. Panadería Rosetta started out as a tiny shopfront in an alleyway with mostly orders to go, but with popularity, it's evolved into a full-fledged Europe-meets-Mexico cafe on the sidewalk. These pastries will blow your mind; try the Guava roll, and you'll see what I mean. And they always have seasonal, limited-edition pastries like a Pan de Muerto covered in black ash (I have constant dreams about that bread) for Dia de Los

Muertos. Oh, and their cafe location they have a breakfast menu with a carnitas sandwich that is to die for. But be warned, this is one of the most sought-after spots in Mexico City, so there will most likely be a line. Don't come if you're starving, and pack a book (and some patience!) for your wait.

Original Location: Puebla
⊙ **Open:** Mon-Sat 7am-8pm / Sun 7:30am-6pm
♥ **Where:** Roma Norte
🏠 **Address:** Puebla 242

Full Cafe Location: Colima
⊙ **Open:** Mon-Wed 7am-9pm / Thu-Sat: 7am-10pm / Sun 8:30pm
♥ **Where:** Roma Norte
🏠 **Address:** Colima 179
@panaderiarosetta

....

RAKU CAFE

A Japanese inspired cafe serving more than great coffee and matcha. You must try the Tamago sando con queso (japanese-style egg sandwich with cheese) and the curry donut. Both sound weird, but I'm asking you to trust me - they're delish. And I know you came to Mexico to experience Mexico…but Asian culture is actually quite a strong thread in the culinary world in Mexico City. Eating here is part of the Mexico City experience and is a nice little break from eating Mexican flavors for every meal.

⊙ **Open:** Mon-Fri 8am-7pm / Sat 9am-7pm / Sun 9am-2:30pm
♥ **Where:** Roma Norte
🏠 **Address:** Sinaloa 188
@rakucafe_mx

....

CAFE MILOU

A must for breakfast or a boozy brunch (the owners also own a wine bar so…). The menu is classic and simple with perfectly executed croissants, quiche, and, yes, even avocado toast. The food and the atmosphere make you feel like you're eating on a corner in Paris… which, strangely enough, is exactly what it can feel like to eat on a corner in La Roma.

Ps. Cafe Milou is right on the border between Roma and Condesa, so most people refer to it as being in Condesa, but its address is actually in La Roma.

⊙ **Open:** Mon-Sat 8am-10pm / Sun 10am-6pm
♥ **Where:** Roma Norte
🏠 **Address:** Veracruz 38
@cafemilou

ABARROTES DELIRIO

Inspired by the New York-style deli, this female-owned and led restaurant is a self-service-Deli where you can buy quality pantry products like freshly made bread and pastries, honey, wine, cheese, and charcuterie, as well as simple to-go meals like sandwiches or Spanish tortilla. Everything is made with and by local ingredients and producers. This spot is perfect for a quick stop before continuing to explore the city or to get something for a picnic somewhere.

⊙ **Open:** Mon -Wed 8am-9pm / Thu-Sat 8am - 10pm / Sun 9am - 7pm
♥ **Where:** Roma Norte
🛗 **Address:** Colima 114
@AbarrotesDelirio

....

LALO!

A casual eatery by the same people behind Maximo Bistrot. At Lalo! Here you'll find Mexican classics like chilaquiles, but also international options like a Croque Monsieur. This is the place for hearty breakfasts and brunches paired with a good coffee or a fresh Agua Fresca. However, if you plan to come on the weekends, come early you'll be stuck in line for a good two hours. That's just how popular this place is.

⊙ **Open:** Tue-Sun: 8am-5pm
♥ **Where:** Roma Norte
🛗 **Address:** Zacatecas 173

STREET FOOD & LOCAL SPOTS

LUIS: CALDOS DE GALLINA & ENCHILADAS

As local as it gets, this little gem tucked away in La Roma serves most soul-warming chicken soup you can find. Seriously, anytime you're feeling under the weather, missing homemade food or find yourself cold in the Mexico City winter and needing a warm meal, come pay Luis a visit. But stick with the pechuga (chicken breast), because you'll soon discover that people will have chicken feet and other more "adventurous" parts of the chicken floating in their soups. They also serve enchiladas and quesadillas with some fun fillings.

Fun Fact! Joaquin Cardoso, chef, and co-owner of Loup Bar, recommended this place to us as one of his favorite eats in the neighborhood, and as his go-to spot to bring other visiting chefs from around the world.

⊙ **Open:** 24/7!

♥ **Where:** Roma Norte

🛑 **Address:** Puebla 188, on the corner with Oaxaca

@caldosdegallinayenchiladas

⊙ **Open:** Mon-Thu 2pm-3am / Fri 2pm-5am / Sat 3pm-5am / Sun 3pm-5am

♥ **Where:** South of Roma Sur

🛑 **Address:** Petén 248 y, Av. Universidad, Narvarte Poniente

....

EL VILSITO

Autoshop by day, taco shop at night. El Vilsito fills up with locals starting around dinner time and gets so packed that cars back into the parking lot and open their trunks to make makeshift places to sit. It feels like a tailgate! When they get super busy, you might have to chase down the waitress who's running around taking orders. It's an exciting kind of chaos! Order the al pastor and a couple of beers while you wait. See a local eating something yummy? I did a lot of pointing and ordering here, in the "I'll have what he's having" sort of way. It works.

But hey, El Vilsito is kinda in the middle of nowhere. You'll have to take an Uber here. And also for that reason, don't go alone. You should have a friend with you. Pss. I went here directly after my Temazcal Ceremony and dropped me back at the meeting point in Roma. Still high off the experience, this place made me feel like this is life.

TACOS LOS PARADOS

Los Parados means the standing ones and in true taco stand fashion...there's nowhere to sit. There's lots to choose from the menu but the costilla (bistec and cecina) are the most beloved. What makes this particular taco so special? Their grill runs on coal, giving everything a smokier taste and a crispier finish.

These tacos are among the best in Mexico City, and during the weekends, they're open 'til 5AM. Stop here on your way home after a night out!

⊙ **Open:** Mon - Thu 12:30pm-3am / Fri-Sat 12:30pm-5am / Sun 12:30am-1pm

♥ **Where:** Roma Sur

🛑 **Address:** Monterrey 333

TACOS EL CALIFA

If you're nervous about street food, start here. Tacos El Califa's menu is more approachable, with mostly beef tacos filled with fancier cuts (like sirloin, flank, and rib-eye) than your regular street taco stand. But the best thing to try here are the "costras", a layer of cheese burned to a crisp that wraps around cheese-covered meat. Basically, the cheese acts like a tortilla. You'll see El Califa locations everywhere, don't be afraid to try!

⊙ **Open:** Mon-Sun 12pm-4am
♥ **Where:** Roma Norte
🏠 **Address:** Álvaro Obregón 174
@elcalifa_mx

ESQUITES DURANGO

This food truck sells delicious and cheap esquites (corn cups) with a wide variety of toppings and salsas. The perfect snack to walk around and explore the neighborhood. Oh, and they even have chapulines (grasshoppers) as a crunchy topping that Emy loves to sprinkle on her esquite.

⊙ **Open:** Tue-Sun 5pm-10pm
♥ **Where:** Roma Norte
🏠 **Address:** Corner of Tonala and Durango

TACOS CARIÑITO

Street tacos with a modern twist! Tacos Cariñito loves to play with the concept of a taco. They are constantly serving special tacos in collaboration with different chefs who might add an Asian element with hoisin sauce or with a Thai twist. They've got beer and wine available, too!

⊙ **Open:** Tue-Sun 5pm-10pm Mon-Sat 2pm-10pm / Sun 2pm-8pm
♥ **Where:** Roma Norte
🏠 **Address:** Guanajuato 53
@tacoscariñito

REPÚBLICA DEL TACO

Chips and guacamole. Tortilla soup. And at least one taco of whatever calls to you. And if it's drinking time, a creative cocktail designed to pair perfectly with anything you choose. That is what you order here. Expect your street taco experience to come with 5-star service and a place to sit this time! República del Taco proves that Mexican street food can be elevated without losing its charm.

⊙ **Open:** Tue-Sun 5pm-10pm Tue - Thurs 1pm -11pm / Fri-Sat 1pm - midnight / Sun 10am - midnight
♥ **Where:** Roma Norte
🏠 **Address:** Colima 220

POLLOS PONCHO

It's no secret I'm obsessed with rotisserie chicken (if you've followed me on Insta for a while, you know). And Pollos Poncho is my go-to chicken spot in Mexico City. Their menu is unpretentious, selling roasted chicken either natural-style or with an al pastor flavor. You can get the whole chicken, a few pieces or even a chicken taco or torta. This place is a pretty cheap and healthy place to eat, but one that will have you licking your fingers. Yum! Ps. you can also order via UberEats, Didi or Rapi.

⊙ **Open:** Tue-Sun 5pm-10pmMon - Sat 10am-11pm / Sun 10am - 9pm
♥ **Where:** Roma Norte
🏠 **Address:** Alvaro Obregon 118
@ pollosponcho

FIUFIU FLAUTERIA

Flautas in a cup. What a concept. FiuFiu Flauteria, as they brag on their Instagram bio, reinvented how we eat flautas. Usually, flautas are something you'd want to sit down for because, well, there's a lot of salsa involved and it can get messy. But here, you get your flautas in a paper cup, and you can dip, eat and repeat on the go. Isn't it brilliant? And it doesn't hurt how fun and colorful this little place is.

⊙ **Open:** Tue - Sat 1pm - 8pm
♥ **Where:** A couple blocks away from Parque Rio de Janeiro
🏠 **Address:** Tonala 36, Roma Norte
@fiufiuflauteria

MEXICO CITY LOCAL TIP
How do you know a street food stand is worth it?

"If you see women there. Because women are way more picky than men. Women won't waste calories on a bad taco."

— ASTRID FROM EAT BY A LOCAL

YES, THOSE LITTLE BLACK THINGS ARE BUGS!

ALEXA'S FAVORITE!

EXPENDIO DE MAIZ

Okay, this place is weird. Everything about Expendio de Maiz is weird, starting from how to get a table to how to eat the food. Pay attention

How to Get a Table: They don't take reservations, but you do need to show up and put your name on a list. You might wait an hour, you might wait four hours. When the host calls you, you better pick up and get your ass to the restaurant within ten minutes, or you will be bumped and have to wait longer. Somehow, this felt like a game that I wanted to win. While you wait, you can go next door to El Parnita or Biergarten.

How to Eat: This restaurant doesn't have a menu. Food just keeps coming. When your plate is finished, they'll ask you if you want another plate. You keep eating until you're full. When you make

a reservation, they might ask you if you have any food restrictions. I recommend being open to eating everything, even bugs.

Every day is different at Expendio de Maiz. One day you'll get a fresh ceviche, and the next, a juicy torta. Each plate is inspired by the owner Jesus' childhood. Ps. Jesus will likely be the one putting your name on the list. Big guy with long hair. And you can taste the love in every one of them.

This place is great for solo foodies. With just a few tables, there's a chance you'll be seated at a table with other guests, and here's a chance to make new friends over a tasting adventure!

⊙ **Open:** Tue - Sun 2pm - 6pm
♥ **Where:** Roma Norte
🏠 **Address:** Yucatan 84
@exp_maiz

CASUAL SPOTS

EL PARNITA

El Parnita is Emilia's go-to spot for bringing foreign friends (like me!) because it's the perfect balance between local and cool. The tacos here are insane. They put a spin on the classics, like a pastor taco made with octopus instead of beef, and they offer imaginative tacos filled with things like crunchy grasshoppers. This should be one of your first eating stops in the city!

🕐 **Open:** Wed 1pm-6pm / Wed-Fri 1pm-11pm / Sat 9am-11pm / Sun 9am-6pm
📍 **Where:** Roma Norte
🏠 **Address:** Yucatan 84
@el_parnita_roma

....

FRITO Y CRUEL

You've gotta come and try the spicy, fried chicken sandwich here, with a side of fries or coleslaw. This is how fancy Mexican people do fast food, and damn it's delicious. To amplify this food experience, pair your sandwich with a cider. Frito y Cruel is a tiny casual corner spot to stop for a quick bite (they've got places to sit) or to order for delivery from the comfort of your own couch via Rappi.

🕐 **Open:** Tue-Wed: 1pm-10pm / Thu-Sat: 1pm-12am
📍 **Where:** Roma Norte
🏠 **Address:** Colima 76-C
@fritoycruel

....

PIZZA FELIX

Located at the end of a hall, behind a conspicuous entrance in Alvaro Obregon, this place often slips under the radar for non-locals. Thankfully, you have this guide, and you know exactly where and how to find my favorite pizza in La Roma.

This spot is as casual as it gets, as it should be for a pizzeria, with lots of plants and colored string lights hanging on the brick walls. The pizzas are thin and crispy and oh-so-good. And as for the drinks, they serve organic wine to pair and cider to sip with your pizza. Pro Tip! Order the Death in Venice… It's a bit spicy, but the best one!

🕐 **Open:** Mon-Wed 1pm-12am / Thu-Sat 1pm-2am / Sun 12pm-12am
📍 **Where:** Roma Norte
🏠 **Address:** Alvaro Obregon 64
@felixpizzabar

BASICO

Farm to bowl! As in many places in Mexico City, Basico is centered around the idea of clean and ethical ingredients. Basico is the Spanish word for basic, and this restaurant is all about just that: going back to basics. The menu is mostly healthy bowls and freshly made bread. You can get things like a Mediterranean bowl with lentils and chicken or a salad bowl with salmon! It's a nice break from the typical diet of tortillas and cheese!

⊙ **Open:** Mon-Fri 8am-10pm / 9am-8pm
♥ **Where:** Roma Norte
🏠 **Address:** Sonora 84
@se_basico

CAFÉ DE NADIE

Music, drinks, food, and coffee. This place is versatile. Famous for its huge collection of records, Cafe de Nadie is a cafe by morning and bar by night. Literally. As soon as the sun goes down, the sign behind the bar lights up, crossing "Cafe" and replacing it with the word "Bar" written in bright neon. The menu's heartline is veggies and fresh produce that is, of course, locally sourced, with dishes like a coconut and watermelon aguachile. But they do have shrimp aguachile and other carnivore options like a scrumptious chicken sandwich. And to drink? They make a mean martini here. Cheers!

⊙ **Open:** Mon 4pm-11pm / Wed-Thu 2pm - 2am / Fri 12pm-2am / Sat 10am-2pm / Sun 10am-12pm
♥ **Where:** Roma Norte
🏠 **Address:** Chihuahua 135

BUTCHER & SONS

Located between two of the most iconic streets in La Roma, Colima, and Orizaba, Butcher and Sons is about burgers, burgers and more burgers. These are some of the best burgers in town, I promise you. Named after famous musicians like Jimi Hendrix and David Bowie, their burgers range from classic to crazy, with ingredients like a fried tortilla and raclette cheese in some of them. And vegetarians, don't fret; they've got burgers for you, too.

⊙ **Open:** Mon-Sun 8:30am-11pm (Brunch menu 8:30am-12pm)
♥ **Where:** Roma Norte
🏠 **Address:** Orizaba 87
@butcherandsons

MERCADO ROMA

I'm just gonna say it upfront, Mercado Roma is popular, but in my opinion, is a little too trendy. But I'm going to write about it because someone is going to recommend it to you. So here we go.

Mercado Roma is a three-story-high upscale food hall filled with small eateries and mini pop-up food stalls from restaurants around town. Just like a food court, you wander around until something catches your eye, and your order and your food are delivered to wherever you choose to sit. I recommend sitting in the back of the food hall if you wanna grab a beer. But if not, I'd recommend the outside tables in the front.

After you eat, head to the top floor where there's a beer garden called, well, Biergarten. They play sports on big screens, and it's a cool spot for a beer or a casual date.

⊙ **Open:** Mon–Wed 9am –10pm / Thu: 9am – 1:30am / Fri – Sat: 9am – 2am / Sun 9am–7:30pm
♥ **Where:** Roma
🛱 **Address:** Queretaro 225
@mercadoroma

INCREDIBLE CULINARY EXPERIENCES

HUGO EL WINE BAR

Date spot alert! Even if you're solo, come here and date yourself with a glass of wine in their sexy bar and their sexy dishes. Their menu is hard to define, with Asian-inspired dishes that mix tuna and kimchi, and others with a more European vibe like their anchovy and radicchio salad (which is my favorite by the way!) Come for a glass of wine and abite, or you can just come for dessert. I don't usually like panna cotta, but this one completely blew my mind.

⊙ **Open:** Tue-Sat 2pm-11pm / Sun 3pm-10pm
♥ **Where:** Roma Norte
🛱 **Address:** Veracruz 34
@hugoelwinebar

FEMALE SAFE ZONES!

Both Hugo El Wine Bar and Loup Bar are safe spot for girls! If you're ever in the area and feel unsafe, come here and approach the staff, and they will help you out. These two places are also perfect date spots. If your date goes wrong, or the guy from Tinder doesn't look like his picture, you these guys have your back!

LOUP BAR

You know a place is good when local chefs show up to eat and drink on their days off. Loup Bar is a favorite for chefs off-duty. The food is high-end but in a very subtle, humble way, with a menu that is constantly rotating according to the season and their unique, all-organic wine selection. They also serve organic cider and other spirits from small (and very innovative) producers. ProTip! The food here is always amazing, but don't miss the mashed potatoes. They're like Christmas in your mouth.

Ps. It doesn't hurt that Emy's sister owns this restaurant. She knows you're coming, and she's waiting for ya with a 10% discount in your bull with the code: **LOUPFLAMINGO** Cheers!

⊙ **Open:** Daily 12pm - 11pm
♥ **Where:** Roma Norte
🛬 **Address:** Tonala 23
@loupbar

FUN FACT! Loup Bar was one of the first places to bring natural wine to the Mexico City food scene. Their wine selection is super unique!

ROSETTA

The mastermind behind Rosetta is female chef Elena Reygadas was recently named the World's Best Female Chef 2023 by World's 50 Best. The Best Female Chef in the entire world!!! This sounds so high-end but Rosetta is set in an old colonial townhouse filled with houseplants and an eclectic and cozy vibe that feels so welcoming. And their menu is very approachable too, centered around the homeyness of Italian flavors, but with a Mexican twist. And since most ingredients are sourced from local producers, the menu is in constant change, but the home-made pasta and risottos are always a must!

◉ **Open:** Mon - Sat 1pm - 12am
♥ **Where:** Roma Norte
🛗 **Address:** Colima 166
@restauranterosetta

MAXIMO BISTROT

One of Mexico City's pioneers of the farm-to-table movement. Their menu is prepared with local and fresh produce grown in the Xochimilco chinampas (the same place with the colorful boats) and nearby areas. It mixes bistro classics like a brioche cheeseburger with Mexican-infused dishes like a roasted octopus with mole.

Maximo Bistrot has become a culinary household name in the city, and you should book ahead in advance! Ps. They have tasting menus which I recommend you try if you're coming for dinner!

◉ **Open:** Mon - Sat 1pm-11pm / Sun 1pm - 6pm
♥ **Where:** Roma Norte
🛗 **Address:** Álvaro Obregón 65
@maximobistrot

EM

What even is this restaurant? Em refuses to define themselves, but you can expect Mexican ingredients with a dash of Asian influence. For example, the star of the show here at Em is the spicy fried chicken, so good that it ended up with its own take-out project (search for @ luchoshotchicken on Insta). You can come here just for the fried chicken, or you can go all out with a tasting menu. Dishes are farm-table and seasonal!

◉ **Open:** Mon - Sat 2pm - 11pm
♥ **Where:** Roma
🛗 **Address:** Tonalá 133
@em.rest

CAMPOBAJA

Ocean to table! Campobaja's menu changes daily depending on the fresh ingredients they can find to feed you! One day they've got oysters with quail egg; other days, it's shrimp tacos. If you love eating here once, keep coming back. Your experience will be ever-changing!

◉ **Open:** Tues-Saturday 1pm-10pm / Sun 1pm-6pm
♥ **Where:** Roma Norte
🛏 **Address:** Colima 124-E
@campobaja

....

MARMOTA

A little piece of my home in Mexico City! Marmota is a restaurant inspired by the Puget Sound, the seafood-dense water channels that run through Washington State. That means come with an appetite for crab, fish, shrimp, and shellfish. The menu serves wild-caught seafood and ingredients directly sourced from local farms. Good people, good food. They deserve your love and support.

◉ **Open:** Tue-Fri 2pm-11pm / Sat 10am-11pm / Sun 10am - 6pm
♥ **Where:** Roma Norte
🛏 **Address:** Plaza Río de Janeiro 53
@marmota

ASIAN FOOD

Ok, I know it seems weird to include an Asian Food section in a Mexico Travel Guide…but there is such a brilliant Asian food scene in Mexico City that it's become part of the culture. Especially in La Roma.

MOG BISTRO

This place has been around for a while, and it's one of La Roma's go-to spots for everything Asian. Sushi, ramen, pad thai…you name it. While I usually distrust places with such varied menus, Mog is the exception. The food is always great and even their Asian-inspired desserts, like their matcha creme-brulee, are wonderful. This place is low-key trendy! One of those places that will make you feel cool and worldly, because girl, you are!

◉ **Open:** Mon-Sun 1pm-12am
♥ **Where:** Roma Norte
🛏 **Address:** Frontera 168
@mogbistro

....

BENGALA

Owned by the same group as Mog, Bengala is their newest addition to their growing family of Asian food spots. Bengala, however, is entirely Chinese food.

They serve dim sum, noodles, Chinese greens and a wide array of Chinese tea.

⊙ **Open:** Mon-Sun 12pm-10pm
♥ **Where:** Roma Norte
🏠 **Address:** Río Pánuco 128

....

BAOBAO

Like its name suggests, this Taiwanese eatery is all about baos. You know, those deliciously fluffy Asian hamburgers stuffed with fried chicken, ribs or beef! They even have assemble-your-own-bao kits. While baos are the main stars of the show, BaoBao also serves up a superb tea-smoked duck and Taiwanese beef noodle soup!

⊙ **Open:** Mon-Sun 1pm-10pm / Sun 1pm-6pm
♥ **Where:** Roma Norte
🏠 **Address:** Guanajuato 202
@baobao_mx

....

IZAKAYA KURA

My favorite Japanese spot in Mexico City. This place is a Japanese Bistro fashioned after a typical after-work bar in Japan, except that you'll find this place full of locals and Mexicans instead. The menu is completely authentic Japanese cuisine prepared with carefully selected, high-quality

ingredients. The place, Rare Sake brands, Japanese Whisky, and many cocktails.

⊙ **Open:** Daily / Lunch 11:30am - 5pm / Dinner 5pm - 12am
♥ **Where:** Roma Norte
🏠 **Address:** Colima 378
@izakaya_kura

SWEETS

HELADO OBSCURO

The name of this place is word play for "The Dark Side," and it's just that: Ice Cream gone naughty! It's ice cream "piquete" (with alcohol), as we say in Mexico. Here you can get your pick of ice cream with Mezcal, tequila, gin, wine, brandy, rum, vodka, and even liqueurs. But since you're in Mexico, try the Tequila or Mezcal. Not a drinker? Don't worry, they have "virgin ice creams," too.

⊙ **Open:** Sun - Thu 12pm - 8 pm / Fri - Sat 11am - 9pm
♥ **Where:** Roma Norte
🏠 **Address:** Orizaba 203
🔲 Helado Obscuro

Drinking Day & Night in Colonia Roma

PARAMO

Right next to El Parnita, there's a random door. Go in and follow a dimly lit flight of stairs, and you'll find Paramo. A low-key bar inside a patio full of plants and color-string lights, and oldies playing. This is the kinda place you want to spend a while kicking back and having a couple of beers. Easy and laid-back, unlike many other trendy spots in the city. Paramo is great for a post-taco-craze downstairs at El Parnita, or to come straight for some of the hibiscus tacos of their own.

⊙ **Open:** Mon-Sun 2pm - 1:30am
♥ **Where:** Roma Norte, right above El Parnita
🏛 **Address:** Yucatan 84
@paramo_roma

....

LA BOTICA

Have you tried Mezcal yet? This is the spot to do it, and do it with a side of orange and crispy grasshoppers if you want to do it right. La Botica place feels like your big brother and

his friends opened their own secret bar and are having a blast goofing off while also nerding out on their cocktails. It's a dive bar but also a hole-in-the-wall that opens up onto the street. Super solo-friendly!

⊙ **Open:** Tues-Thus & Sun 5pm-midnight / Thurs-Sat 5pm-2am
♥ **Where:** Roma Norte
🏛 **Address:** Orizaba 161
@laboticamezcaleria

....

LA DOCENA

When you're in the mood to absolutely drink with your meal, make this place a priority. La Docena is New Orleans meets Mexico with savory Po Boys and fresh aguachiles. La Docena means "The Dozen," and it refers to how oysters are sold by the dozen.

Mainly an oyster bar, this place is famous for all the seafood and its single dessert: a dulce de leche molten cake with banana ice cream. This dessert is so scrumptious it feels almost sensual. This is a great spot to grab a late lunch or an early dinner and a few drinks. Pro Tip! The fries here are to die for; ask for some of their homemade aioli and dip away!

⊙ **Open:** Mon - Thu 12pm - 10:30pm / Fri-Sun 12pm-11pm
Where: Roma Norte
Address: Álvaro Obregón 31

@ladocenaoysterbar

GIN GIN KITCHEN BAR

Yes, this is a Gin bar. Gin Gin is inspired by the idea of gin as a remedy more than a drink. The menu has a wide selection of gins and gin concoctions that make a gin and tonic sound boring. Dimly lit but very lively, this place feels mysterious and evokes a feeling of euphoria. Gin Gin is the exact middle ground between fancy and casual. The bar is stunning, and it's the coolest place to sit. This place has become such a staple that they have two locations only in La Roma. Pro tip! Order a Mexican Pimm and some pizza.

⊙ **Open:** Mon-Sun 1pm-2am
Where: Roma Norte
Address: Cordoba 107

CONTRAMAR

Day drinking anyone? Frequented by influencers and businessmen alike, Contramar is almost a cult in Mexico City. 2 p.m. on a Friday, and this is the place to be for a long lunch and a few rounds of drinks. The food is casual: tuna tostadas with chipotle mayo galore, spicy aguachiles, pastor fish tacos, and so on.

While the food is casual, the setting is not. The tables are fully dressed in crisp white linens, and the servers are donned with bow ties. Come here to kick off the weekend. Just don't forget to book your table in advance!

⊙ **Open:** Mon-Fri: 12pm-8pm / Sat-Sun: 11am-8pm
Where: Roma Norte
Address: Durango 200
@contramarmx

HOTEL CASA AWOLLY

Get ready: this place is not just a bar; it is a whole aesthetic experience. Inside a beautiful old mansion (you're in La Roma, after all), Casa Awolly is vibrant and colorful, and exciting. It is a perfect mix of gastronomy, mixology, and architecture. The menu includes high-end Mexican snacks, and the dishes are so photo-worthy. Upstairs you'll find a shaded rooftop bar serving incredible cocktails. You'll leave energized and more in love with this colorful city than you already are.

⊙ **Open:** Tue-Sat 9am-1am / Sun 9am-7pm
♥ **Where:** Roma Norte
📷 **Address:** Sinaloa 57
@casa_awolly

COCKTAILS &NIGHTLIFE

BAR LAS BRUJAS

Get your full-black outfit ready and head to Bar Las Brujas for a witchy night of potion-inspired cocktails in a sexy and mysterious ambiance. This place is one of my go-to spots for a cocktail whenever I'm in Mexico City. It's the only bar in the city with an all-female staff, and its menu is an almanac of unique cocktails with herbs and natural ingredients, all inspired by women in history who were labeled as witches. And to make it even more special, Las Brujas is located in the legendary "House of Witches", an elegant mansion from the early 1900s that got its name not

because it's haunted but because of its pointy rooftops that resemble a witch's hat, and that looks like it was taken straight out of a witches tale.

⊙ **Open:** Tue - Sat 5pm - 2am / Sun 5pm - 12am
♥ **Where:** Steps away from Parque Rio de Janeiro
📷 **Address:** Calle Rio de Janeiro 56

MAISON ARTEMISIA

One of the sexiest bars in Mexico City, if you ask me. Artemisia is the idyllic urban bar, an evocative and intimate space to come for a cocktail and be transported to a bohemian Paris in the 1920s. They specialize in Absinthe and botanical cocktails, but they're masters of the classics, like good old Old Fashioned. If you're having a hard time deciding what to order, try the Salmocito, a sweet and tangy gin-based cocktail with grapefruit. Maison Aremisia is right above Loup Bar, so you can easily slip upstairs for a nightcap after your dinner.

⊙ **Open:** @brujasmex
♥ **Where:** Right above Loup Bar
📷 **Address:** Tonala 23

JARDIN PARAISO

Formerly known as Cafe Paraíso, Jardin Paraiso reopened last year and is now another great place to come for a night of dancing! Latin meets electronic beats. This place is one of the go-to's in La Roma for going out, and it can get packed, so arrive before 11:30pm to make sure you get in.

Ps. There's a huge neon flamingo inside! Don't forget to tag me in your pics!!!

NOTE: There's a $200 pesos cover for walk-ins, $100 pesos cover for bookings.

⊙ **Open:** Thu 12am-4am / Fri-Sun 12am-5am
♥ **Where:** Roma Norte
🛏 **Address:** Querétaro, next to Mercado Roma
☐ **Contact:** + 52 55 1289 0129

DEPARTAMENTO STUDIO BAR

This is always where the party is. Why? Because it's chill and comfy and makes you feel like you're back in college hanging at a friend's place…except that friend has turntables playing electronic music with a few hits here and there. I don't usually like electronic music, but here it's not overwhelming, so you can have an actual conversation. Grab a beer or two or some mezcales and enjoy!

⊙ **Open:** Wed-Thu 6pm-12am / Fri-Sun 2pm-1am
♥ **Where:** Roma Norte
🛏 **Address:** Álvaro Obregón 154
@departamento_studiobar

MAMA RUMBA

Best salsa dancing spot in town! Owned and run by a Cuban, Mama Rumba is where you come to dance your heart out to a live salsa band while sipping mojitos. If you are one of those people who can stay up past 10pm, this place is a must in your Mexico City adventure. And the best part: free salsa dancing lessons on Thursdays right before they open. Go to Girls in Mexico City and assemble a group of girls for a dancing night out! Ps. Mama Rumba is cash only.

⊙ **Open:** Wed-Sat 9pm - 3am
♥ **Where:** Roma Norte
🛏 **Address:** Queretaro 230
◼ Mama Rumba Roma

Things to Do & See in Colonia Roma

WALK AROUND

Buy a coffee at Buna (or anywhere) and take a stroll around Plaza Rio de Janeiro and go from there. Explore the neighborhood, do some window shopping or actual shopping in all the cute little stores around. La Roma is made for walking and all the things to do, see and eat are within the same radius. Put your earbuds and tune into our Mexico City playlist ☞

SIGHTS ON BIKES - AIRBNB EXPERIENCE

If you're like me and have got the attention span of a squirrel, then you might find it more enjoyable to see all the sights with a tour guide that can quickly point them out to you, give you sufficient insight and move on. That's why I like this tour that takes you to "20+ Must-See Sights" on a bike! Book this tour for one of your first days in Roma Norte and afterwards, you'll have a good understanding of the area and what to do with the rest of your time here.

BONUS: As this is a group tour, you have a good chance of making some friends. Don't be shy to ask them to get a bite to eat later that night (I do that all the time on tours). Say, "I'm going to _____ this evening, feel free to join me!"

🏷**Budget:** $44 USD

Look for Sights on Bikes on Airbnb or go here ☞

ATTEND A COOKING CLASS WITH SOBREMESA

What better souvenir than a new set of skills? Sobremesa offers classes with the masters behind many of the coolest restaurants around the city. No workshop is ever the same and their class roster is always changing. One week it's learning how to make traditional tamales, and the next there's a class about Jewish Babka bread. So visit their website to check upcoming classes and events to see if any appeals to you! Check them out at ⊕sobremesa.mx

🎟 **Budget:** Depends on the class
📍 **Where:** Roma Norte
🏠 **Address:** Puebla 125
@sobremesa.mx

ADMIRE THE BEAUTIFUL CASA LAMM

Casa Lamm is La Roma's most iconic landmark and one of its original occupants. Built in 1911 as a private residence, it was never actually inhabited by its owners - but it didn't go to waste. Casa Lamm was turned into a school, then abandoned and brought back to life in 1993 as a Cultural Center. They have a gallery with great rotating exhibitions, and they offer a wide range of workshops and academic studies. All art and culture related, of course.

🕐 **Open:** Mon - Fri 9am - 3pm
📍 **Where:** Roma Norte
🏠 **Address:** Alvaro Obregon 99

VISIT MODO - THE OBJECT MUSEUM

In a city full of museums, this one is an unexpected pivot. MODO tells the untold story of the life behind everyday objects. Make-up, toys, soda bottles, religious figurines, cameras, all kinds of objects that will give you a glimpse into a different kind of Mexican history: the history of daily life. It holds a collection of over 150,000 objects from the early 19th Century to the present day, both common and exotic. This is the perfect plan for a rainy day in La Roma!

Budget: $50 pesos

Open: Wed-Sun 10am-6pm

Where: Roma Norte

Address: Colima 145

CHECK OUT GALERIA OMR

Follow the artsy vein of this city in Galeria OMR, one of the most respected galleries in town. It showcases both emerging and established artists for over 30 years and it's known for its cutting edge exhibits. There's always something cool and thought-provoking on display.

Open: Tue - Thurs 10am - 7pm / Fri 10am - 4pm / Sat 11am - 4pm

Where: Roma Norte

Address: Cordoba 100

@galeriaomr

ESCAPE FROM AN ENIGMA ROOM

This is not for the faint of heart. If you've ever wanted to feel like the star of an action (or horror) movie, Enigma Rooms will fulfill that dream. These live-action escape rooms are inspired by major films, and every experience is thoroughly curated to make you forget you're in a pretend scenario. Their experiences range from mild, like solving a mystery a la Sherlock Holmes, or facing a serial in a gorey, Saw-inspired room. In every experience, you have 60 minutes to solve the challenge and free yourself. You need a minimum of 2 to book one of their experiences, so if you're solo you're going to need to assemble your girl gang. Head to our Facebook group, Girls in Mexico City, and invite some gals to join you. There's no bonding like the one that is created while trying to deactivate nuclear missiles as an undercover CIA agent. Ps. This might require some Spanish, but it's fine if you're not that fluent!

Budget: $250 pesos

Open: Daily 10:45 am - 9:30pm

Where: Roma Norte (more locations with different experiences!)

Address: Colima 385

Shopping in Colonia Roma

MERCADO DE MEDELLIN

The official name of this market is Melchor Ocampo Market, but it's more simply known as Mercado de Medellin because it's located on Medellin street. And funnily enough, it's full of Colombian products, as well as items from all over Latin America. It's sometimes also called "Little Havana"

With over 500 stalls, this market is one the Roma residents go-to markets. Groceries, dry goods, produce, seeds, spices, flowers, you can find it all. Plus, other non-essentials like craft beer. And of course, a myriad of food stalls with yummy chilaquiles, tacos, tamales, and all the Mexican goodies you can dream of. Language Tip! "Puesto" means "stall".

⊘ **Open:** Daily 8am - 6:30pm
♀ **Where:** Roma Norte
🛕 **Address:** Medellin 20

BAZAR DEL ORO

A little weekend market selling Mexican crafts. Come here for some souvenir shopping if you don't want to go all the way downtown. Besides crafts, you'll find a few food stalls serving from traditional quesadillas to Spanish paella.

⊘ **Open:** Sat-Sun 9am-10pm
♀ **Where:** Roma Norte
🛕 **Address:** Callejon El Oro S/N (very close to La Cibeles Roundabout)

LA LAGUNA

La Laguna is technically in the next neighborhood, called Doctores, but it's so close to La Roma that it's basically Roma-adjacent. This space is an abandoned lace factory turned into a collective project that houses cool projects and entrepreneurs in different fields. Here you'll find temporary art exhibits as well as niche shops and even a tiny mezcal bar in the courtyard. These are a few of the things you'll find inside...

→ **Loofok Selections,** the natural wine shop that co-owns Loup Bar (page 145). Come here for tastings or to buy some bottles.

→ **La Metropolitana,** a Mexican brand that creates contemporary furntiure inspired by iconic and classic design pieces.

→ **The New Sanctuaries,** a beautiful brand selling skincare products and candles inspired by astrology. Created and run by Tatiana, a lovely girl from Colombia.

→ **Buna's cafe roastery**...and a bigger cafe to come and sip some coffee.

→ **Anfora,** a table service manufacturer that has been around for 100 years. If you want to buy beautiful, traditional yet contemporary plates and dishes to beautify your kitchen, this is where.

📍 **Where:** Roma-Adjacent

🚉 **Address:** Dr. Lucio 181

VINTAGE SHOPS

You've got some killer vintage shopping opportunities in La Condesa. Get ready for some real daring style finds.

Here are some boutiques to visit:

♥ **Void -** For luxury vintage shopping

♥ **Goodbye Folk -** For a sea of lost, retro jewels

♥ **Vintage Hoe -** For an affordable fashion trip back in time...and a fun name.

CHAPTER TWO

La Condesa

THE VIBE:

Whimsical, safe and charming

BEST FOR:

Sitting at cute cafes and taking long strolls under the trees

DAYS NEEDED:

2 or 3, but it's easy to stay longer

La Condesa

Back to the NYC comparison game: La Condesa is often compared to NYC's Soho District.

POV: You're sitting on a sunny terrace, having a frothy cappuccino, and reading a book. The weather is nice, and the streets are filled with laidback fashionable people walking their dogs. You've got no plans except dinner plans, and you're perfectly alright with that.

La Condesa is a leafy oasis in the middle of the concrete chaos that this city can be. This neighborhood is similar to La Roma, with art deco buildings covered in ivy and avenues lined with trees - but La Condesa has more of a boho vibe to it. Think of La Roma as the trendy, urban younger sister, always on the hunt for the next it-thing. And of La Condesa, like the more laid-back hippie-ish older one, who is really cool but in a subtle, almost accidental way. It is a vibrant yet calm neighborhood, dripping in greenery that hovers over the cozy cafés, modern bistros, and chic hangouts sprinkled along its streets.

Before Roma became cool, Condesa was the trendiest neighborhood back in the early '00s. And way before that, it was the poshest and most cosmopolitan area back in the 1930s, home to the artistic upper class.

Areas to Know in La Condesa

AVENIDA AMSTERDAM

Originally a horse racetrack, the "Hipodromo Condesa" street is still a loop that follows the course. In this city, things aren't taken down and replaced. Here, life layers are on top of former life layers. And this avenue, I dare say it's one of Mexico City's loveliest streets. There's a passageway in the middle of the street lined with trees and plants all along the way. Or you can wander on the sidewalk and window shop as you stroll. This street is full of cafes and fun shops for you to peruse around.

PARQUE MEXICO

This 9-hectare park is one of the city's lungs and one of the main attractions for your visit. Not because there's particularly anything to see (unless you're an architecture buff and you'll marvel at the Art Deco monuments), but because it's such a quintessential Mexico City experience to walk through it, coffee in hand and just watching life go by. The park is always alive, full of joggers, friends catching up, doggie school, dance classes, skateboarding classes, and kids flying off their heads as they breakdance to a small, gathering audience…this not-so-little park is a whole universe of its own.

PARQUE ESPAÑA

Smaller than Parque Mexico, but even more green! Parque España is full of murals, sculptures, fountains, and people taking refuge in the cool shade. And, of course, it's also full of people and their dogs.

AVENIDA MAZATLAN

Life usually happens on Avenues Michoacan and Amsterdam, but Avenida Mazatlan is one of the most interesting streets to walk along when in La Condesa. The median that runs along the street is wide and bursting with greenery. There's nothing bucket-listy here, but if you're a fan of walking along pretending you're the main character in a romance film, you'll understand this vibe.

✎ **TRAVEL NOTES:**

....

....

....

....

....

....

FUN FACT!

Condesa means "countess", and it's named after the Countess of Miravalle, who owned the land in colonial times. This place is literally made for women.

Where to Eat in La Condesa

COFFEE & COWORKING

BLEND STATION

This cafe is a digital nomad's dream. Spacious laptop-friendly tables, fast Wi-Fi, and a beautifully designed space will keep you inspired throughout your work session. I love that there's a tree in the middle of the courtyard, which adds an extra touch of calm. All their coffee is Mexican - but you can have it anyways you want! Ask one of their "coffee geeks" (that's what they call their staff!) for recommendations!

⊙ **Open:** Daily 8am - 8pm
♥ **Where:** Condesa (but they also have locations in Roma and Polanco!)
🏠 **Address:** Tamaulipas 60 / Amsterdam 282
@blendstation_

QUENTIN CAFE

Come sit at the bar and watch coffee being crafted or bring your laptop and focus. While most cafes in Mexico City sell just Mexican beans, Quentin Cafe does not discriminate. You can try and taste coffee from all around the world. Their original location is in Alvaro Obregon avenue in La Roma, but I like this one so much better. The place is comfy, with a touch of quirky found in the brass monkeys hanging upside down scattered around the room. Oh, and try the pastries. They always have incredibly delicious pastries.

⊙ **Open:** Sun-Wed 8am-10pm / Thu-Sat 8am-11pm
♥ **Where:** Condesa
🏠 **Address:** Amsterdam 67a
@quentincafe

BREAKFAST & BRUNCH

MOLINO EL PUJOL

If you had to choose just one place to come for breakfast, I'd say choose this one. Modeled after a traditional tortilleria, Molino El Pujol is another one of the super famous chef Enrique Olvera's brainchildren. But unlike its older, fancier siblings like Pujol and Quintonil, "El Molino", as it's commonly called, is a modest, straightforward eatery serving simple tacos like an avocado taco in a blue corn tortilla pressed with hoja santa (a large leaf considered sacred in some indigenous cultures) and some Mexican snacks like esquites with a chicatana ant mayo. The mayo is made with crushed ants, and it's amazing, trust me. While you're here, order the "agua de cacao" to drink. It's cacao water. Also amazing.

By the way, Molino El Pujol really is a tortilleria, and it's where all the tortillas for Olvera's other restaurants are made, so you can buy tortillas by the kilo to take home. The place functions as a small "abarrote" or convenience store where you can buy an assortment of products too, like their incredible salsas.

A TACO MADE WITH A TORTILLA PRESSED WITH A LEAF CALLED HOJA SANTA AND FILLED WITH AVOCADO, NEXT TO AN EPAZOTE QUESADILLA. THIS LOOKS VERY SIMPLE, BUT I PROMISE YOU IT'S HEAVEN!

⊙ **Open:** Daily 9am - 7pm
♥ **Where:** Condesa
🏠 **Address:** General Benjamin Hill 146
@molinopujol

LA ESQUINA DEL CHILAQUIL

Probably one of the most famous corners in Mexico City, if not the most famous, thanks to one dish: the torta de chilaquiles. Yup, you read that right. A torta filled with chilaquiles. Who thought of this crazy idea? No idea, but it turned out brilliantly. This street stall may be tiny, but it's the definition of mighty. The line can circle all around the block, and they sell a crazy amount of tortas every morning. They sell out rather quickly, so come early.

⊙ **Open:** 8am - 12pm
♥ **Where:** In the corner of Tamaulipas and Alfonso Reyes
📛 **Address:** Alfonso Reyes 139

CHILPA

Mexican brunch anyone? This is one of the best spots to come for chilaquiles. Here you get to build your own chilaquiles where you pick the sauce, the tortilla chips, the protein, and the toppings. Plus, they have a custom-made, signature salsa prepared with 5 different types of chiles... You can also try other Mexican breakfast classics like huevos rancheros (yum) or molletes (double yum), but the chilaquiles are my fav.

⊙ **Open:** Mon - Fri 8am - 6pm / Sat - Sun 9am - 5pm
♥ **Where:** Condesa
📛 **Address:** Chilpancingo 35
@chilpa_mx

SAINT

Right next to Molino El Pujol, there's a charming little bakery called Saint where the bread is fantastic. Even Emy's brother-in-law, a French wine and food expert, is obsessed with this place. If there's anything French people know, it is bread. You've never tried a croissant as perfect as this one (unless you've been to Paris, then disregard my previous statement). The place works mostly as a bakery where you come, shop, and go, but there are a few small tables on the street right outside where you can sit and make love to your pastry.

⊙ **Open:** Mon-Sat 7:30am - 8pm / Sun 8:30am - 7pm
♥ **Where:** Condesa
📛 **Address:** General Benjamin Hill 146-1
@saintpanaderia

LARDO

European and Mexican fusion cooked in a wood-burning oven. Here you'll find dishes like Mexican chilaquiles with a European twist of gooey burrata instead of Mexican cheese! It's gourmet, it's casual, and the restaurant makes you feel like you're dining somewhere in the countryside instead of the concrete jungle, which is a nice break. The bakery here is the same as Rosetta in La Roma, so delicious pastries are a must. Get the fruit tart with ice cream; it counts as breakfast because there's fruit in it.

Ps. This place is by Elena Reygadas, the female chef powerhouse behind Rosetta in La Roma.

⊙ **Open:** Mon/Sat 7:30am-11pm / 7:30am-5:30pm
♥ **Where:** Condesa
🚇 **Address:** Agustín Melgar 6
@lardomexico

....

MAQUE CAFÉ

I'd also recommend Maque for a Mexican breakfast. A quaint, old-style traditional restaurant right on the corner of Parque Mexico, with freshly-made pan dulce (Mexican pastries). Your choices will be vast, but don't leave without trying an iconic concha, a traditional Mexican soft, sweet bread covered in sugar in a turtle-shell-like pattern. If you want to eat your concha like a Mexican, order a hot chocolate to dip it in!

⊙ **Open:** Mon - Sat 8am - 10pm / 8am - 9pm
♥ **Where:** Condesa, in the corner of Ozuluama and Citlaptepetl
🚇 **Address:** Ozuluama 4
@maquecafe

....

OJO DE AGUA

After all these heavy breakfasts, you're going to want something light eventually! This is where the active girls make a pit stop after their yoga or cycling classes for a juice or a smoothie bowl. Ojo de Agua also has salads and sandwiches filled with greens and nutritious proteins. This place is a bit more pricey compared to the brunch spots, but hey, it will keep you fuller longer. Think of it that way.

⊙ **Open:** Daily 7am - 10pm
♥ **Where:** Condesa, almost right on the corner of Parque Mexico
🚇 **Address:** Citláltepetl 23
@ojodeaguamexico

TACOS HOLA

You want a really local taco? This place has been around for decades and is an OG on-the-street taco scene! Tacos Hola serves guisado tacos (check the taco glossary in page 48) that taste like you're eating in the home of a Mexican family. Plant-based friends, this is the taco spot for you. They have many vegetarian and vegan-friendly taco options! Oh, and even though it's a local spot, they have English menus. Your brain can take a break from all the translating.

⊙ **Open:** Mon-Fri 9am-9pm / Sat 9am - 8pm / Sun 9am - 3pm
♀ **Where:** Condesa
🛖 **Address:** Amsterdam 135
@tacosholaelguero

EL TIZONCITO

This recommendation came from Emy's dad, who was born and raised in Mexico City! Shout out to Francisco! So, El Tizoncito claims they invented the Pastor taco, and we're gonna them the benefit of the doubt. Holding true to the traditional al pastor taco, El Tizoncito is one of the last taquerias that still cook the "pastor al carbon" (with coal), giving it a delicious, crispy finish to the meat. My mouth is watering as I write this. And now you can say you've tasted the original pastor taco.

Ps. These guys also have many locations around town, so keep an eye out.

⊙ **Open:** Daily 12pm - 3am
♀ **Where:** Condesa
🛖 **Address:** Tamaulipas 22
@eltizoncito_oficial

TAQUERIA ORINOCO

Travelers and locals alike love this retro street taco spot. In fact, it's one of the most visited taco shops in the city, and for good reason. They serve true northern-style tacos, tacos norteños, which are ah-mazing. Tacos norteños are bigger, meatier and cheesier. My kind of taco! Order a Campechana, a taco filled with a mix of beef AND pastor. Two delicious worlds in one. Ps. They have several locations around the city.

⊙ **Open:** Daily 1pm - 11pm
♀ **Where:** Condesa
🛖 **Address:** Yucatán 3
@taqueriaorinoco

EL GRECO

El Greco has been serving tacos since the '70s, and it's an institution in La Condesa. It tends to be filled with locals seated at a wobbly table that is probably-50-year-old devouring their Arab-style signature taco called the Doneraky. This is their most-ordered taco which consists of fluffy pita bread instead of a tortilla filled with pork pastor. If you've already tried one-too-many pastor tacos, come to El Greco for this specialty.

⊙ **Open:** Mon-Wed 2pm - 10:30 pm / Thu-Sat 2pm - 4am

♀ **Where:** Condesa

📛 **Address:** Michoacan 54

LUNCH & DINNER

MEROTORO

An A-list restaurant and one of Condesa's top places to eat according to any Mexican foodie you ask. MeroToro is part of Latin America's 50 Best Restaurants, and this place hasn't stopped buzzing since it opened in 2010. What's all the fuss about? MeroToro serves high-end, Baja-style surf and turf. For surf, you've got incredible seafood and for turf, get ready for more exotic meats like rabbit and wild boar, which highlight the wildness of Baja! And since Mexico's wine country is in Baja, you'll also find Baja wines from Baja vineyards.

⊙ **Open:** Mon-Sat 1:30pm-11pm / Sun 2pm-10pm

♀ **Where:** Condesa

📛 **Address:** Amsterdam 204

@merotoromx

MALCRIADO

One of the newest additions to La Condesa, Malcriado is where coffee and wine meet. It is an easy and unpretentious place designed to chill and hang out while having comforting, simple, yet high-end and delicious food. Malcriado, which translates as Spoiled, embodies the essence of la Condesa: casual vibes with a touch of rebellion; of doing things your way and enjoying life. My favorite things about this place? Their side-walk communal bench and stools where you can sit with your glass of wine and watch the cool Mexico City crowd flutter by.

⊙ **Open:** Wed - Mon 8am - 10:30pm

♀ **Where:** 10 min. Walk from Parque España

📛 **Address:** Atlixco 127

@malcriadocafe

CIENA

Having lunch on a sunny day at the streetside tables of Ciena perfectly represents the true Condesa experience. The menu at Ciena is small but perfectly curated. A calamari and clam risotto, fresh pasta with braised lamb, a catch of the day crusted in citrus salt… there's no wrong choice when it comes to ordering here. And for dessert, don't miss their cheesecake. The only downside of Ciena is that, even though it's in a beautiful corner, it's also a noisy one with lots of street venues and musicians…or is that an upside?

⊙ **Open:** Mon - Sat 8am - 10:30pm / Sat 9am - 5:30pm
♥ **Where:** Condesa
🛋 **Address:** Alfonso Reyes 101
@ciena____

....

PASILLO DE HUMO

It's time you try some Oaxacan food, a cuisine known for its smoked meat! This signature smokiness is where the inspiration for this restaurant was born. Pasillo de Humo could be translated as "smoke alleyway"referring to the market passageways where beef would be hung up to be smoke-dried. This smokiness is also ever present in mole, a dish that comes from Oaxaca! Popular dishes here include the mole, of course, and also the plantain croquettes and tlayudas.

⊙ **Open:** Mon - Wed 9am - 10pm / Thu - Sat 9am-11pm / Sun 9am - 7pm
♥ **Where:** Condesa, in the Parian Condesa Hall
🛋 **Address:** Nuevo Leon 107
@pasillodehumo

....

CEDRÓN

Mediterranean classics in a beautiful environment. This is your sanctuary when you need a breather from Mexican flavors. Cedron's chef, Alejandro Fuentes, opened this place after seven years of traveling and working as a private chef, mostly at sea in the Mediterranean, and his years as a sous chef at the Ritz in Paris. His menu is a selection of international dishes, like eggs benedict for breakfast and an impeccable Coq Au Vin for lunch or dinner. But I recommend trying the Onion Soup Burger with raclette cheese!

⊙ **Open:** Daily Breakfast: 8am - 12:30pm / Lunch 2:pm - 11pm
♥ **Where:** Condesa
🛋 **Address:** Mazatlán 24
@cedron_condesa

MILO'S

A cozy european-inspired joint with beautiful interiors and tasty bites. Come here for a late lunch and a glass of wine or for dinner on a Friday or a Saturday night to listen to live Jazz (music starts at 8:30pm!). Milo's has a bit of a romantic feel to it that makes it perfect for a date, either a coffee date during the day, or during the night for a more romantic atmosphere.

⊙ **Open:** Daily 8am - 11pm
♥ **Where:** Condesa
🏛 **Address:** Amsterdam 308
@miloscondesa

SWEETS & DESSERT

CHURRERIA EL MORO

This churro shop has been around since 1935. Opened by a Spanish guy back then, legend has it that this is where and how churros were introduced to Mexico - by Churreria El Moro. This spot has remained a family business ever since and has grown to be an icon. Their Condesa location, while not the original one, is one of the most famous ones. It sits in a charming corner right across Parque Mexico, and the beautiful white and blue tiles on the walls have made El Moro a quintessential #InstaSpot.

My recommendation? Order your churros, some hot chocolate, and take a stroll around the park.

⊙ **Open:** Sun - Thu 8am - 10pm / Fri - Sat 8am - 11pm
♥ **Where:** Facing the East side of Parque Mexico
🏛 **Address:** Michoacan 27
@churreriaelmoro

··

NEVERIA ROXY

Another cult-classic in Mexico City! Neveria Roxy has been around since 1946 and, to this day, is still run by the same family! And that's what you'll love about this place - not just the delicious ice cream but also the retro vibes and family feeling that comes with it. It's old school. Stop by Neveria Roxy after lunch for some "nieve" (water-based ice cream), and I recommend you try the Mamey flavor, a fruit that you will unlikely find anywhere else and that tastes something in between a peach and a baked sweet potato. It's rich, creamy, and perfect for dessert.

⊙ **Open:** Daily 11:30am - 8:30pm
♥ **Where:** Condesa
🏛 **Address:** Fernando Montes de Oca 89
@neveriaroxy

Drinking Day & Night in La Condesa

FELINA

This bar feels like a little secret. Dimly lit, full of vintage couches and jazzy vibes with great cocktails and killer tunes. Felina is so laid back, perfect for a solo drink or a Bumble date. They have a wide rum-based selection of cocktails, all the classics like an Old Fashioned done perfectly and some imaginative twists like a Mezcal Sour. They've nailed it.

⊙ **Open:** Tue-Wed 6pm-1am / Thu-Sat 6pm-2am / Sun 6am-10pm
♥ **Where:** Condesa
📫 **Address:** Ometusco 87
@_f_e_l_i_n_a

....

LA XAMPA

Bubbles, bubbles, and more bubbles. La Xampa is all about the fizz, focusing on cava, champagne, prosecco, and sparkling wine-based cocktails. Heaven, basically. Even though an all-bubble bar sounds glitzy and glam, this place is actually very unpretentious and

relaxed. It has a classic European look and a super long bar that I prefer to sit at. They also have a few snacks to help you soak up all the champagne. And for your friends who don't like to have fun, they have a non-bubbly menu too.

⊙ **Open:** Daily 1:30pm - 3am
♥ **Where:** Condesa
📫 **Address:** Nuevo León 66
@la_xampa

....

CAIMÁN

You know how wine is always thought to be a pinky-up kinda thing? Well, this is one of those places that defies that idea. Caimán is all about casual vibes and good chats around the bar, like when you're hanging around a friend's place on a summer day, drinking and snacking while time flies by.

Come here for a spritz or a petnat (the term for natural bubbly wine!) and to snack on some of their canned goods, like Spanish mussels, sardines, and olives. Who knew canned food could be so fun and trendy?

Ps. If you're a fan of the Aperol Spritz like me, try the Caimán Spritz, their own adventurous version of the Aperol!

⊙ **Open:** Wed - Sun 5pm - 2am
♥ **Where:** Condesa
🏠 **Address:** Av. Nuevo León 120
@caiman_bar

....

BALTRA

Where off-duty bartenders come for a drink (that's how you know it's good). That place is Baltra, a little bar just a few blocks away from Parque Mexico. But don't judge this place by its size, what they lack in space, they make up for in their incredible cocktails! They serve classic drinks but they also have a rotating menu of their own liquid inventions. I recommend skipping the classics and asking for the bartender's recommendation for a unique drinking experience. Oh, and hey, Baltra ranked #32 in the 2022 Bar Edition of World's 50 Best, juuust in case you needed a little more convincing to stop here for a cocktail or two.

⊙ **Open:** Sun-Tue 6pm - 12am / Wed 6pm - 1am / Thu - Sat 6pm - 2am
♥ **Where:** Condesa
🏠 **Address:** Iztaccíhuatl 36-D
@baltrabar

....

TRAPPIST

My boyfriend is a big beer nerd, so whenever he comes along on my adventures, we have one mission: to find the craft beer! And he wants to try local craft beer from that region. We found success at Trappist, a small beer bar and brewpub serving small-batch craft beers. Craft beer is always more expensive than local beer, so expect to be paying prices similar to home instead of Pacifico prices - but I've learned that when you travel, finding craft beer is synonymous to finding the coolest locals in the most unsuspecting hole-in-the-wall spots. Craft beer hunting is now one of my favorite ways to get off the tourist path around the world, Trappist included.

⊙ **Open:** Mon-Sat 12pm-8pm / Sun 12pm-6pm
♥ **Where:** Condesa on the Hippodrome
🏠 **Address:** Av. Álvaro Obregón 298
@eltrappist

Things to Do in La Condesa

TAKE A STROLL AROUND PARQUE MEXICO

The best thing you can do in La Condesa is just walk around and take it all in. Head to El Moro for some decadent churros and a hot chocolate, and head across the street to the park for a stroll.

...OR PARQUE ESPAÑA

You can walk all the way from Parque Mexico to Parque España, or you can head directly to Parque España for a different walk. You can bring a book and sit at a cafe somewhere or just people-watch.

DOG-WATCHING

Forget people-watching and get ready for all the furry friends. I swear it seems like 8 out of 10 people in Mexico City have dogs because you see so many people walking around with them, having coffee with them, chilling at their feet, and running around for playtime. If you're a dog lover, you'll go crazy here.

Fun Fact! If you see a bunch of dogs lined up, just laying there, chilling, you just stumbled upon a dog school, and class is in session. Lots of people drop their dogs off at doggie school while they go to work, so their fur babies can be properly trained and educated instead of lazy and disobedient. Brilliant!

CATCH A SHOW AT FORO SHAKESPEARE

A stage for independent plays and performances where you can catch all kinds of shows: stand-up comedy, wacky and funny lucha libre satires, and even concerts. Watching a full play in Spanish sounds daunting, but it'll be the best language immersion experience to continue practicing your español.

🎟 **Budget:** From $350 pesos
📍 **Where:** Condesa
🏛 **Address:** Zamora 7
Check out their roster at foroshakespeare.com

MEZCAL TASTING WITH AN ARTISANAL PRODUCER

Look for this exact title on Airbnb Experiences. Here is where you learn all about Mezcal, tequila's smokey cousin. You'll learn how to sip mezcal with an expert and since this is a group experience, it's also a great way to meet some other travelers while getting slightly buzzed.

If you can't find him on Airbnb, you can message the host, Mario, on IG: @Mezcalman

🎟 **Budget:** $60

CHURROS MASTERCLASS WITH CHEF

Another Airbnb Experience to search for (I love AirbnbExperiences)! This one is all about the churros from scratch, baby. Cooking skills are the best souvenir to bring home - especially when you're making a dish with easy-to-find ingredients like churros! You'll also learn how to make hot chocolate from scratch, which is the perfect pairing.

 Search Churros Masterclass with Chef on Airbnb or @ricardo_lopez_x on Instagram

🎟 **Budget:** $23
Psst. Ricardo also has a coffee-tasting Airbnb experience, too.

Shopping in La Condesa

LA CONDESA'S TUESDAY TIANGUIS

A weekly market set up on the west side of La Condesa where you'll find all kinds of produce, proteins, groceries, and cheese. All the local cheese! This is one of Emy's favorite markets in Mexico City because, unlike other markets, it's never too crowded. Emy says she used to do all her grocery shopping with her sister here - and she'd always stop for a tostada with sour cream and Oaxaca cheese at a local stand. Take a morning stroll through this market, buy yourself some fresh juice and sample some Mexican snacks along the way.

⊘ **Open:**Tuesdays 10am - 5pm
♀ **Where:**West Condesa
🏛 **Address:** Pachuca 13

ISMOS

Come here to shop one-of-a-kind handcrafted contemporary Mexican jewelry from over 100 designers. You can find silver, gold, crystals, and a mix of all of the above. With so much silver and metals, Mexico is known for its craftsmanship in jewelry, so this is a great spot to pick some gifts to take home. Or to choose a memento for yourself to remember this amazing trip.

⊘ **Open:** Mon - Fri 12:30 - 6:30 pm / Sat 12pm - 5pm
♀ **Where:** Condesa
🏛 **Address:** Campeche 410

San Miguel Chapultepec

THE VIBE:

Residential and Quiet

BEST FOR:

Gallery hopping

DAYS NEEDED:

One day - or two at the most

San Miguel Chapultepec

Welcome to this mini-chapter dedicated to San Miguel Chapultepec, a tiny quarter bordering La Condesa. Why is this small area worth including? Well, mostly because it is your gateway to Chapultepec Park and all the treasures among the trees.

But also because it's calm and feels pretty local, with pedestrian-friendly streets and families walking around. It's also one of the city's established "cultural hot zones" with most of the city's best galleries.

While other areas attract visitors like moths to a flame, San Miguel Chapultepec is quietly cool.

FUN FACT! Chapultepec means grasshopper in Náhuatl, the language of the Aztecs. Chapultepec Park has been an important landmark for hundreds of years!

Where to Eat in San Miguel Chapultepec

COFFEE & COWORKING

CAFEVERA

You are home at this dreamy little cafe where you'll want to bring your journal, laptop or book and be in no hurry at all! The owners of Cafevera Calavera are so friendly and welcoming - and they speak English which can be a relief after a few days of stumbling through Spanish (you're doing great, don't worry). The incredible coffee is just the cherry on top! Really, come here for the atmosphere and hospitality, and you'll be rewarded with amazing cappuccinos - and even delicious crepes - made with love!

⊙ **Open:** Mon-Fri 8am - 9pm / Sat 9am - 9pm / Sun 10am - 7pm
♥ **Where:** San Miguel Chapultepec (one block from the park)
🖬 **Address:** 11850 Ciudad de México
@cafeveramx

MARNE CAFÉ

A place for coffee and bread lovers. Marne Cafe was born as a specialty coffee shop, then later expanded into a bakery and incorporated a brunch-friendly menu that includes bites like a cured salmon bagel and grilled cheese. But also some more elaborate dishes like braised ribs with mashed potatoes. However, I wouldn't order anything without bread at Marne! It's all about the bread.

Ps. Marne's french toast is among the best in the city.

⊙ **Open:** Mon - Fri 8am - 8pm / Sat - Sun 8am - 9pm
♥ **Where:** Polanco
🖬 **Address:** Emilio Castelar 212
@marne_mx

CAFE PAPAGAYO

It's breakfast all day at Cafe Papagayo! Tables on the street make Cafe Papagayo a great spot to wake up with a cup of coffee and breakfast with a twist. Try the french toast with mascarpone, their BLT with kale instead of lettuce, or their chilaquiles made with blue corn tortilla chips. If you're hungover, go for the massive breakfast burger.

⊙ **Open:** Mon-Wed 8am - 7pm / Thu - Sat 8am - 9pm / Sun 9am - 2 pm
♀ **Where:** San Miguel Chapultepec
📮 **Address:** Gobernador Ignacio Esteva 51B
@cafe_papagayo

LUNCH, DINNER & LOCAL SPOTS

PANIFICADORA ERMITA

Local pastries at local prices (that's code word for cheaper than you'll find at the fancy cafes). This is a classic Mexican bakery with fresh goodies in the window, which you cannot help but stop and drool at. This is a good place to grab a bite to walk with or to gently stuff in your purse for later. But beware, these pastries are huge! If you ask,

"Que me recomiendas?" (what do you recommend) just make sure they don't hand you an entire loaf of bread.

⊙ **Open:** Daily 5am
♀ **Where:** In front of José Morán y Vicente Eguia colonia
📮 **Address:** Jose Vasconcelos 124

....

TACOS MORAN

This place is so local that they serve your food on a plate wrapped in a plastic bag for fast and easy clean up. You show up, order your two tacos or torta, eat at your plastic table and chairs, and keep it moving. That's the authentic experience! And hey, if you haven't tried a volcano yet, this is the place to do it. The menu is in English, so you can be a little adventurous without accidentally ordering something too outside your comfort zone...because, yes, they do have tongue tacos.

⊙ **Open:** Mon-Sat 3pm - 1pm
♀ **Where:** San Miguel Chapultepec
📮 **Address:** C. Gral. José Morán 71-local-A
@tacosmoran

COMAL OCULTO

A casual little corner with some of the best "antojitos mexicanos" (Mexican snacks) around! This place is owned by the sweetest couple, and they treat it like it's their home. And everything on the menu is and tastes indeed homemade. When you visit, you must try their Flautas in Salsa Verde...or better yet, order them "divorciadas" so you get to try both the salsa verde and salsa roja (red salsa). After your meal, order a Cafe de Olla and one of their handmade cookies and continue exploring the neighborhood!

⊙ **Open:** Mon-Fri 10am - 6pm / Sat 10am - 5pm
♀ **Where:** San Miguel Chapultepec
🖈 **Address:** Gral. Gomez Pedraza 37
@comaloculto

MARI GOLD

Mari Gold is the Mexican Indian fusion you didn't know you needed in your mouth! The cuisine here can be described as daring, if not rebellious! And it works! For example, if you like fish tacos and fish and chips, you'll love the fried fish bun drizzled with achaar mayo (like tartar sauce but better). If you're not a fried fish person, I feel sorry for you - but anyways, order their chicken wings, kebabs, sandwiches - really anything. If you like big flavors, you can't go wrong here.

GOOD TO KNOW: Many of their dishes can be made gluten-free!

⊙ **Open:** Wed - Monday 10am - 5:30pm
♀ **Where:** San Miguel Chapultepec
🖈 **Address:** Protasio Tagle 66A
@mari.gold.mx

What to Do in San Miguel Chapultepec

Art and history lovers, get ready…

BOSQUE DE CHAPULTEPEC

The second largest city park in Latin America and Mexico City's biggest green lunch is Bosque de Chapultepec. This area is centered around Chapultepec Hill, which is crowned with Chapultepec Castle! Back in pre-colonial times, this park was a retreat for Aztec rulers. Nowadays, it's a retreat for locals to enjoy time in nature, have picnics and naps beneath the trees, do yoga, work out, and take a breather from the busy streets.

This park is also home to three iconic museums: the Anthropological Museum, the Tamayo Museum, and the Museum of Modern Art. There are so many things to do in this park that it could have its own chapter of its own, but really, here's what are the highlights to get you started…

Ps. This Park also holds the Chapultepec Zoo, but I don't recommend it at ALL.

CASTILLO DE CHAPULTEPEC (CHAPULTEPEC CASTLE)

A local and national landmark, this castle is also commonly known as the National History Museum - as its walls are brimming with history. It was originally a military school, later on, the home of valiant leaders like Emperor Maximilian of Habsburg and later o,n, President Porfirio Diaz. Since royalty actually lived here, that makes Chapultepec Castle the only real castle in North America.

The castle has been restored to its original design with checkered floors, chandeliers, stained glass window panes, and opulent decor in general. The museum displays artifacts from and by ancient Mexican cultures, from the Revolutionary War and murals by iconic painters from the early 1900s. The castle overlooks Paseo de la Reforma Avenue, making it one of the best viewpoints in the city. The view alone is one of the reasons people make it up the hill!

If you plan on visiting this castle (I think you should!) I have two pieces of advice. Number One: Get the audio guides, they cost $3 USD and take you on a much deeper journey of knowledge than what you'd experience without them. My second piece of advice is to come early! Since the pandemic, the castle now has a limit of 10,000 people per day. Which sounds like a lot, but you'd be amazed…

🖋 **Budget:** $80 pesos (free but busy on Sundays)

⊙ **Open:** Tue-Sat 9am - 5pm

ᘖ **How to get here:**

Follow the road that leads upwards behind the Monumento a Los Niños Héroes (big white building with many marble columns in a semicircle). If you don't feel like walking, you can take the mini-train-like vehicle that runs up every 15 min for just 25 pesos for a roundtrip and feel like a toddler at the mall.

LAGO MAYOR

As you walk around the park, you'll find a lake with a big fountain in the middle. This lake is known as Lago Mayor. It's a leisurely space where people come for a jog or a walk and where families come with their kids on the weekends. You can rent kayaks and pedal boats for as cheap as $40 pesos.

LAGO / ALGO

A pandemic baby, this building was formerly known as "Restaurante del Lago" - and it has now reopened its doors as a two-sided project: LAGO, which encompasses a cafe and restaurant; and ALGO, a gallery that displays temporary exhibits of all kinds of artistic disciplines. You can pop by to have a bite to eat, but if you want to visit the gallery, you must book in advance. Book your visit at:

⊕ lagoalgo.setmore.com/bookappointment

⊙ **Open:**
LAGO / Mon - Wed 8:30 - 7pm / Thu - Sat 8:30am - 11pm / Sun 8:30am - 6pm
ALGO / Wed - Sat 10am - 7pm / Sun 10am - 6pm
♀ **Where:** By the Lago Mayor
🏛 **Address:** Bosque de Chapultepec S/N

MUSEO DE ANTROPOLOGÍA (THE ANTHROPOLOGY MUSEUM)

When I first came to Mexico City, this was the #1 attraction recommended to me by literally everyone I asked for recommendations. Welcome to the world's largest collection of ancient Mexican art! Museo de Antropología takes you on a journey from the indigenous tribes of the Americas through all the cultures that developed in Mesoamerica.

Now, there are two things you need to know before you go:

❶ First, this museum is huuuge, so plan to spend at least a few (fascinating) hours here.

❷Second, the displays and information are mostly in Spanish. There's not a lot of information in English here. And so, I recommend a hiring guide to bring this museum to life for you - even if you speak Spanish, actually.

🎟 **Budget:** $85 pesos
⊙ **Open:** Tue-Sun 9am - 5pm
📍 **Where:** Bosque de Chapultepec
🏛 **Address:** Paseo de la Reforma S/N

REALLY, GET A GUIDE.

I loved the Anthropology Museum, but I wished I had gone with a guide. As I don't speak history-Spanish (I more so speak food-Spanish), I was a little lost at times and wished I could have dove a little deeper into the significance of some of the storylines in this museum.

So I recommend either going on a tour like this:

Or hiring a local guide. You will spot local guides outside the museum when you approach.

MUSEO TAMAYO

If you're into modern and contemporary art, you can't miss this museum. Its exhibits are known for being innovative and avant-garde! Plus, they have an ever-growing permanent collection of gems too. This museum is a quicker visit, too - I'd say around an hour.

🎟 **Budget:** $80 pesos
⊙ **Open:** 11am - 5pm
📍 **Where:** Bosque de Chapultepec
🏛 **Address:** Paseo de la Reforma 51

MUSEO DE ARTE MODERNO

Contemporary and modern art by national and international artists. Museo de Arte Moderno is often overlooked in favor of Museo Tamayo, but I'd recommend this one first as it showcases exemplary Mexican artists like Diego Rivera, José Clemente Orozco, David Alfaro Siqueiros - and Mexican female artists like Remedios Varo and Leonora Carrington!

🖉 **Budget:** $70 pesos / $3.5 USD / Free on Sundays

☉ **Open:** Tue - Sun 10:15am - 5:30pm

♥ **Where:** Bosque de Chapultepec

🏛 **Address:** Paseo de la Reforma and Gandhi S/N

GALLERY HOPPING

The gallery scene in San Miguel Chapultepec is the best. You can start with some coffee in Cafe Papagayo, then hit the exhibits and finish with dinner at Marigold. These are the ones to check out:

→ Kurimanzutto Gallery

→ Enrique Guerrero Gallery

→ Galeria RGR

→ Saenger Gallery

→ Patricia Conde Gallery

→ Labor Gallery

→ Galeria de Arte Mexicano (GAM)

TOUR LUIS BARRAGAN'S WORK

*Casa Gilardi

Nestled in this residential area you'll find one of the most special houses built by Pritzker prize-winning architect, Luis Barragan. If you've never heard this name before, Luis Barragan is Mexico's most influential architect. Do you know how there's this shade of pink that's always associated with Mexico? Well, it's called Barragan pink!

Casa Gilardi is a true hidden gem tucked away in this neighborhood. Why is this house so special? It is the last project Barragan completed before he died. It exemplifies his work, playing with so much color, texture, and light. This house is not open to the public (people live there!), so tours are by appointment only. If this is something you definitely want to do, book your tour ahead at:

⊕ https://casagilardi.mx/?lang=en

✉ casagilardi@gmail.com

🔖 **Budget:** $300 pesos / $15 USD

☉ **Open:** Mon - Sat 10am - 2pm / Sat 10am - 1pm

♀ **Where:** San Miguel Chapultepec

🏛 **Address:** General Antonio León 84

Ps. There's a special fee for taking photos, and only cellphones are allowed, no cameras!

✳Casa Barragan

Luis Barragan's home and studio is not far away, and you can also visit it. It's just as he left it, and tours are provided by enthusiastic architecture students that will share more about his life and point out all the corners and details of the house!

🔖 **Budget:** $400

☉ **Open:** Mon-Fri 11am 5 pm / Sat-Sun 11am - 2pm

♀ **Where:** Facing the Bosque Chapultepec, almost across the street from Papalote Museo del Niño

🏛 **Address:** General Francisco Ramirez 12

Book your tour at casaluisbarragan.org/eng/

Shopping in San Miguel Chapultepec

SUPERCOPE

Locally sourced and locally made Mexican products like salsas, coffee, chocolate and groceries, yummy things to fill your pantry with back home.

⊙ **Open:** Daily 11am - 7pm
♀ **Where:** Right next to Marigold
🛕 **Address:** General Antonio Leon 31

EXPENDIO DOMÉSTICO

A cute little boutique with typical objects used in daily life in Mexico, but re-designed in a contemporary fashion. Glasses, candles, notebooks, cleaning tools, and a whole bunch of curiosities. Come here for not-so-typical souvenirs of your trip to Mexico City.

⊙ **Open:** Mon - Fri 11am - 7pm / Sat - Sun 11am - 4pm
♀ **Where:** San Miguel Chapultepec
🛕 **Address:** General Cano 42

FUN FACT! Chapultepec Park is one of the oldest urban parks in the world.

CHAPTER FOUR

Colonia Cuauhtemoc, Zona Rosa & Juarez

THE VIBE:

Eating. If you find a hotel you love, the benefit is that you're staying near La Roma, but not in the buzz of La Roma!

BEST FOR:

These 3 neighborhoods are just off the beaten path (with sometimes cheaper prices) and have their own eclectic personalities!

DAYS NEEDED:

2-3 nights

Colonia Cuauhtemoc, Zona Rosa & Juarez

This chapter is a 3x1, as these areas are basically together but have personalities of their own. Here's a breakdown for you, so you can easily navigate this area:

→ **Colonia Cuauhtemoc** is a teeny-tiny neighborhood just between La Roma and Ave. Reforma. This area is a cosmopolitan neighborhood that used to be Mexico City's business district. Now it's home to some foreign embassies and, in total contrast to La Roma, many modern skyscrapers. Including Torre Mayor, the tallest building in Mexico.

Colonia Cuahutemoc is also home to the iconic Angel de la Independencia Monument. As La Roma becomes increasingly crowded, many people have started migrating here, and new little gems have sprouted in the past couple of years, making it a new hot area for eating and dining out.

→ Right below Colonia Cuauhtemoc, you'll find **Colonia Juárez:** the new up-and-coming neighborhood that, some say, is becoming the new Roma. But Juárez has been cool in its own way since the 1960's when it became populated by artists and intellectuals. Nowadays, Juárez is getting trendier by the day, as new bars and restaurants pop up in freshly renovated opulent mansions. But as trendy Juárez is becoming, it still feels local, guarding its intellectual tint and urban bones. And finally…

→ **Zona Rosa**, which is officially a part of Colonia Juárez, but it's a whole different Universe. Juárez has a "too cool for school" vibe, with its trendy bars and cool kids running the show, but Zona Rosa is the colorful, eccentric, rhine-stone-studded, feather-wearing twin sister, as it is the LGBTQ+ capital of Mexico City. Needless to say, this area can be fun. Zona Rosa means "Pink Zone", so it's not as debaucherous as a Red Zone, but still an area with some color in its cheeks. Play safely if you go out at night in this area.

Area Breakdown

Colonia Cuauhtemoc and Colonia Juárez are two small triangles that lay opposite each other, divided by Ave. Paseo de la Reforma.

→ **Colonia Cuauhtemoc** is outlined by Circuito Interior Melchor Ocampo to the left side and James Sullivan Street to the right side. It is neighbored by Colonia Anzures and San Rafael.

→ **Colonia Juárez** is outlined by Ave. Paseo de la Reforma, which marks the division between Juárez and Cuauhtemoc. And by Ave. Chapultepec to the left side and Ave. Insurgentes to the right side. It is bordered by La Condesa and La Roma.

→ Same as **Colonia Juárez**, Zona Rosa is also outlined by Paseo de la Reforma, Ave. Chapultepec and Ave. Insurgentes. But Ave. Florencia marks its finish line within Colonia Juárez.

More than areas to know, here are some landmarks that will help you navigate these two areas like a pro.

ESTELA DE LUZ

Easy to spot, this tall rectangle-like monument stands right in the intersection where Colonias Cuauhtemoc and Juarez begin, right after Bosque de Chapultepec.

FUN FACT! Locals call the Estela de Luz monument "la suavicrema", becasue it resembles Mexico's version of sugar wafers. Google it and you'll se what I mean!

AVENIDA PASEO DE LA REFORMA

This wide avenue is one of the city's main veins. It runs diagonally through the city and was built in the 1860s modeled after the big European avenues of the time. It crosses Bosque de Chapultepec and becomes wider right where Colonias Cuauhtemoc and Juárez begin, serving as a divider between the two.

ANGEL DE LA INDEPENDENCIA

Standing right in the middle of Avenida Reforma, you'll find one of the most iconic sights and landmarks of Mexico City: a 118-foot-tall column crowned with a golden statue that is another 22 feet tall. Imposing and grand, this monument towers over the roundabout that separates both neighborhoods. It was inaugurated in 1910 to commemorate the Centennial of the War of Independence and has been witness to many historical moments and events in Mexico City.

FUN FACT! Despite its name, the statue on the top is not really an angel. It's actually a Roman deity called Victoria holding a laurel wreath and a broken chain to symbolize victory and freedom. She also has a sister monument in Paris in the Place de la Bastille that celebrates the victory of the French Revolution.

AVENIDA CHAPULTEPEC

Running parallel to Ave. Reforma, Ave. Chapultepec marks the division between Colonia Juárez and both La Condesa until it hits Glorieta de Los Insurgentes...

GLORIETA DE LOS INSURGENTES

...which works as an elbow that divides Colonia Juárez from La Roma and Zona Rosa.

Where to Eat in Cuauhtemoc, Zona Rosa & Juarez

COFFEE & COWORKING

FARMACIA INTERNACIONAL

A young and fresh vibe in an intimate setting, this spot is great for a little laptop time. Their menu is an assortment of great coffee, biscuits, sandwiches, salads, sweets..and the most beautiful latte! And you must try the homemade pop tarts.

⊙ **Open:** Mon - Fri 8:30am - 8pm / Sat - Su 8:30am - 5pm
♥ **Where:** Juarez
🚇 **Address:** Bucareli 128 F
@farmacia.internacional

....

CHIQUITITO CAFE

Chiquitito Cafe has been around for 10 years and is a favorite in the city. You can order your latte with practically any type of milk, including plant-based milk, and it will be served to you at your breezy street-side table! The coffee is superb, but the dirty chai is the best I've tried in the city.

⊙ **Open:** Mon - Sat 7:30 - 8:30pm / Sun 8:30 - 7pm
♥ **Where:** Juárez (with locations in Roma and Condesa too)
🚇 **Address:** Río Lerma 179
@chiquititocafe

....

CUCURUCHO CAFE

Coffee beans from Chiapas and Oaxaca plus ninja-skilled baristas make Cucurucho famous. That and their pasties. Try the chia and lemon cake and/or the carrot cake! There is a little bench in front of the cafe where you can sit and sip - or take your goodies to go. Cucurucho Cafe isn't the cheapest around, but if you're willing to spend an extra $1 or $2 on artisan coffee and organically made treats, it's worth it.

⊙ **Open:** Daily 7am - 8:30pm
♥ **Where:** Cuahutémoc
🚇 **Address:** Río Nazas 52
@cucuruchocafe

LA RIFA

Ok, this is not a coffee place, but it's something even better! La Rifa is completely dedicated to artisanal Mexican cacao, in every form you can imagine. You can order your chocolate caliente (similar to a hot chocolate but made with mexican chocolate called cacao), which is either water based or milk based, hot or cold, and you can choose your size. They sell chocolate bars and some chocolate-based snacks like chocolate tamales and ice cream! If you can't function without your daily dose of caffeine, order a Moka or a cortado with chocolate foam.

⊙ **Open:** Daily 8:30am 9pm
♥ **Where:** Juárez
🏠 **Address:** Dinamarca 47
@larifachocolateria

PRO TIP! Follow @hereforthecoffeemx - an Instagram page dedicated to the aesthetic of Mexico City coffee shops and coffee shops only.

BREAKFAST & BRUNCH

NIDDO

Crafted by mother and son Karen Drijanski and Eduardo Plaschinkski, Niddo has become THE breakfast/brunch spot in the area. This menu was entirely inspired by their travels, offering you an eclectic spread of choices! The most famous item on the menu is the grilled cheese, but other adored options include the Babka French Toast, shakshuka and eggs, and the falafel burger! And beyond the food, this cafe is the definition of cute. The open kitchen really makes you feel like you're eating breakfast in their family home.

⊙ **Open:**

Breakfasts / Mon - Fri 8am - 1pm / Sat 8am - 2:30pm
Lunch / Mon - Fri 1:30pm - 5:30pm / Sat 3pm - 5:30pm
Brunch / Sundays 8am - 5:30pm
♥ **Where:** Juárez
🏠 **Address:** Praga 24
@niddomx

CAFÉ NIN

If it's a boozy brunch you're looking for, Cafe Nin has got an entire "morning cocktails" section on their menu. The chandelier lighting, brick wall interior, hidden nooks, intimate setting, and jazzy music practically beg you to start drinking. It's never too early for a glass of rose to go with your ricotta lemon roll. If you're a beer drinker, I recommend trying the Carta Blanca Michelada (bonus: it's cheap).

⊙ **Open:** Mon - Wed 7am - 9pm / Thu-Sat 7am - 10pm / Sun 7am - 6pm

♥ **Where:** Juárez

🏛 **Address:** Dresde 2

@cafe_nin

....

BAD!

An acronym for Breakfasts All Day! Get it? At BAD!, you will find all the classic breakfast darlings like fried egg sandwiches, avocado toast, and fluffy pancakes - but if you're in the mood to get a little wild, try the waffle sandwich. No matter what you order, you'll be happy with the portion size! This place doesn't mess around.

⊙ **Open:** Mon - Fri 8am - 3pm / Sat - Sun 9am - 3pm

♥ **Where:** Juárez

🏛 **Address:** Dinamarca 50

@breakfastmakesushappier

STREET FOOD & LOCAL SPOTS

STREET TAMALES

You've heard of street tacos, but have you ever heard of street tamales?! This spot is a secret, hidden gem that I only learned as a recommendation from my chef friends. Come and order the tamal oaxaqueño verde; it's my favorite tamal in the world. It's filled with spicy shredded chicken and green salsa.

⊙ **Open:** Mon . Sat 8am - 12:00pm

♥ **Where:** Juárez, on the corner of Marsella and Dinamarca

🏛 **Address:** Marsella 30

....

EL TACOMOVIL

It doesn't get more local than a Mexican man making tacos out of a little cart that he wheels to and from this spot daily. This taco mobile has incredible guisado tacos: tacos filled with different stews like chicharron in green sauce or green peppers with cheese (rajas con queso). If you want to order a taco that is more familiar to you, stick with some "pollo" (chicken) or "bisteck" (beef). But besides the great food, this place is a beyond-local experience because it has a language of its own, using some slang to list items on their menu. They call their salsa "baptism" because it's so spicy that it's a whole spiritual experience. Last thing: this place has one very important rule… when you get here, you have to ask "quien es el último?" (who is the last one?), so Don Miguel, the owner, can follow on who's next in line for their tacos.

☉ **Open:** Mon - Fri 9:30am - 5pm
♥ **Where:** Cuauhtemoc
🛵 **Address:** Río Pánuco 23
🚩 El Tacomovil

DON VERGAS

Probably the most coveted seafood in Mexico City. The chef is from northern Sinaloa and prepares fresh ceviche and aguachile in his native land's coastal style. You can also try some of the freshest and largest oysters and scallops around. But one of my favorite things here is the Soft Shell Crab Tostada, a hard tortilla shell with shredded crab, a dish that's originally from Mazatlán (a beach in Sinaloa and Emy's hometown!) Don Vergas has become such a cult favorite that on Sundays, there can be up to a 2-hour wait to eat here. Skip the line and book through OpenTable.

☉ **Open:** Mon-Thu 1pm-8pm / Fri-Sun 11am-8pm
♥ **Where:** Cuauhtemoc
🛵 **Address:** Río Lerma 185
@donvergasmariscos

TACOS "EL CAPOTE AZUL"

If you haven't tried carnitas tacos yet, this is the perfect place to do so. What are carnitas again? Yummy pulled pork that is either boiled or fried is used to fill tacos or tortas. Carnitas usually consists of different parts of the pig, but if you don't want any fatty or weird-textured chunks, just ask for "tacos de maciza", which means they'll serve you the leaner parts of the meat. Add some lime and some salsa, and enjoy.

☉ **Open:** Daily 8am - 8pm
♥ **Where:** Zona Rosa, right in the intersection of Ave. Chapultepec and Ave. Insurgentes Sur
🛵 **Address:** Ave. Chapultepec 317 Local 7

BIRRIA COLORADO

The BEST birria tacos in Mexico City. In true birrieria fashion, Birria Colorado serves soft and crunchy tacos but only only only with beef. The special taco to order here is the quesabirria! This is a glorious taco filled with birria AND gooey cheese. One bite and your life will never be the same. And if that wasn't enough...they have pizza birria here. I haven't been as brave to try, but if you do, please let me know how it goes!

⊘ **Open:** Tue - Thu 12pm - 12am / Fri - Sat 12pm - 2am / Sun 10 am - 12 am

⚲ **Where:** Cuauhtemoc (but they have a location in Roma too!)

🏛 **Address:** Río Lerma 218

@birriacolorado

LUNCH & DINNER

MASALA Y MAÍZ

Have you ever eaten something somewhere you've just never gotten over? This is that kind of place. Masala y Maíz is the lovechild of chefs Norma Listman (Mexican) and Saqib Keval (Indian and of East-African descent). The name makes sense when you understand that the menu here celebrates the unexpected similarities between Mexican and Indian food. Their menu is an explosion of creativity and color, mixing the best of both worlds in dishes like Mexican esquites with turmeric and dahlia flower alioli.

⊘ **Open:** Wed - Mon 12pm - 6pm

⚲ **Where:** Juárez

🏛 **Address:** Marsella 72

@masalaymaiz

TAVERNA

Often referred to as Taverna en Prim, this place is inspired by classic European tavernas and how they serve as meeting points to gather with friends and enjoy a good time. Naturally, their menu is designed with sharing in mind. You'll find a mix of mouth-watering Mediterranean appetizers and entrees, but the real reason to come here is for the atmosphere. Set in an old house from the early 1990's and dressed up in rustic decor with mismatched chairs and vintage maps on the walls, I'd dare say this is one of the prettiest restaurants in the city. Note: There's a different menu for the dining area and the bar, if you want a full meal, make sure you book your table at the dining area.

⊘ **Open:** Tue - Wed 1:30pm - 12am / Thu - Sat 13:30am - 1am / Sun 1:30pm - 7pm

⚲ **Where:** Juárez

🏛 **Address:** General Prim 34

@tavernaenprim

CICATRIZ CAFE

Cicatriz Cafe has become iconic in La Juárez. Cicatriz is the work of the American sibling duo Jake and Scarlett Lindemann. Jake, who's also a food photographer, leads the mixology bar. And Scarlett, originally a food writer, leads the kitchen. They've combined their creativity in their respective fields to create a menu that feels planned yet spontaneous. Dishes here are as simple as roasted carrots with tahini and "salsa macha" - and as complex as a chicken and chorizo pie. My favorite? The kale salad. It changed my perception of kale forever.

⊙ **Open:** Daily 9am - 10pm
♀ **Where:** Juarez
🏛 **Address:** Dinamarca 44
@cicatrizcafe

....

AMAYA

Stunning atmosphere and stunning food - Amaya was the pioneer in making La Juarez relevant and cool again. Focused on natural wine and farm-to-table Baja-style dishes, Amaya's menu is sexy and exciting. Try the ragu gnocchi, clam ceviche, or the fried soft-shell crab. And good news for my gluten-free friends, Amaya uses gluten-free flour, so you can go to town on some fried food

FUN FACT: This restaurant was recently featured on Netflix's Somebody Feed Phil.

⊙ **Open:** Mon - Wed 2pm - 10pm / Thu - Sat 2pm - 11pm
♀ **Where:** Juárez
🏛 **Address:** General Prim 95
@amayamexico

....

ROKAI

Sushi anyone? I love a tiny Japanese restaurant where you can sit at the bar and watch the chefs masterfully prepare your meal as you sip some sake. This place is #intimate. Most of the fish served in Rokai is from the Mexican coast, which means that it's super fresh and in comparison to sushi prices in the US, it's a bargain!

⊙ **Open:** Mon -Sat 1pm - 11pm / Sun 1pm - 7pm
♀ **Where:** Cuahutémoc
🏛 **Address:** Río Ebro 87
@rokaimexico

....

ROKAI RAMEN

Not a huge sushi fan? Right next door to Rokai you'll find its twin sister: Rokai Ramen. Another tiny joint that will transport you to Japan but instead of sushi, their menu focuses on - no surprise here - ramen! If you want the best of both worlds, however, you can order some maki here too, and have a ramen-sushi feast.

⊙ **Open:** Mon -Sat 1pm - 11pm / Sun 1pm - 7pm
♥ **Where:** Cuahutémoc
🏠 **Address:** Río Ebro 89
@rokairamen

....

COMEDOR LUCERNA

A bright and splashy food truck park/picnic place where you can taste all kinds of different fare. Pizza, seafood, burgers, popcorn, ice cream - you name it. On the weekends, there's always live music, whether it's a DJ or a jazzy quartet.

This spot is perfect for solo travelers to come and roam, and it's also my recommendation to gather up a group of travel sisters from Girls in Mexico City and have a night out.

BONUS: The facade is always covered with murals that change seasonally. They're always Mexican-inspired and make the perfect backdrop for the prettiest selfies.

⊙ **Open:** Mon - Wed 8am - 11pm / Thu - Sun 8am - 2am
♥ **Where:** Juárez
🏠 **Address:** Lucerna 51
@lucerna_comedor

....

HAVRE 77

Another spot by Eduardo García, the same chef behind Maximo Bistrot and Lalo! (both in Roma), Havre 77 follows Maximo Bistro's recipe for a French-style brasserie - just way more casual. The menu is small but full of French favorites like steak frites, escargots, fresh oysters, and incredibly juicy burgers in brioche buns. For dessert, don't miss the tarte tatin.

And if the food wasn't alluring enough, the space itself is gorgeous. Havre 77 is also the name of the building, a once-derelict construction that was rebuilt, restored, and brought back to life. Don't be surprised if you see influencers and fashionistas using this building as a backdrop for photoshoots, but don't worry, they won't disrupt you; they'll only entertain you from afar.

⊙ **Open:** Mon - Sun 2pm - 11pm / Sun 1pm - 5pm
♥ **Where:** Juárez
🏠 **Address:** Havre 77
@havre77

LUNCH & DINNER

JOE GELATO

Italian gelato with Mexican and experimental touches created by the talented Joe, a young chef who has worked in many renowned restaurants around the world! Unsurprisingly, his ice cream parlor is nothing short of exceptional. This place serves very unusual ice cream flavors like pickle sorbet, marigold, and black garlic - turning ice cream into a gourmet experience. Flavors on the menu are always changing, so just show up and be ready to be surprised. If your palette is not feeling that adventurous, you can always go with more usual flavors like cacao (but hey, live a little).

⊙ **Open:** Tue - Sat 12pm - 7pm / Sun 12pm - 6:30pm
♥ **Where:** Cuahutemoc
🛕 **Address:** Versailles 78
@joegelatomx

CHURRERÍA EL MORO

Sophisticated churros but still Mexican churros! Treat yourself to the upscale version of Mexico City's favorite dessert with classic churros with caramel dipping sauce or the granddaddy of all churro creations, the Churro Ice Cream Sandwich! But, but, but if you're going with the classic churros, get a milkshake to pair it with. Ps. You don't have to wait til after dinner to have churros. This place is busy all day. A small wait is usually required, but it's worth it.

⊙ **Open:** Mon - Fri 8am-10pm / Sat-Sun 8am - 11pm
♥ **Where:** Cuahutemoc (close to Birria Colorado) - there are multiple locations, but I like this one
🛕 **Address:** C. Río Lerma 167
@churreriaelmoro

Drinking Day & Night in Cuauhtemoc, Zona Rosa & Juarez

HANKY PANKY COCKTAIL BAR

A true speakeasy. The location of this place will not be disclosed until you make a reservation. And no, they won't give you the address even then. You will simply receive instructions on where to go and what to look for. I won't say more so I don't spoil any of the fun. But once you've found it, you'll walk into a dimly lit, gaudy, and luxurious space. Head to the bar and watch the bartenders do all the magic. They usually enjoy talking to customers and recommending which cocktail to try. If you had to choose just one nightlife experience in Mexico City, I'd say Hanky Panky is a great choice. Not only is the experience unique, but so are the cocktails. This place is also #13 in World's 50 Best Bars 2022 list, even more guarantee that this place is worth it!

PRO TIP! Leave with plenty of time before your reservation because finding Hanky Panky will be a bit of a scavenger hunt. However, because of this very scavenger hunt-like experience, I wouldn't recommend coming here alone after dark. Gather some friends in Girls in Mexico City and let the fun begin.

⊘ **Open:** Tue - Sat 5pm - 2am / Sun 5pm - 12a,
♀ **Where:** Juárez
Reservations at hankypanky.com

....

TOLEDO ROOFTOP

Located on top of a building, Toledo Rooftop is a green oasis and the perfect stage to watch the sunset or to have a drink with a view of the Reforma Avenue skyline. They play upbeat House music and often have A-list guest DJ's (like Poolside and Chromeo!), and the crowd is always cool. If you want to have a bite with your drink, their menu mixes Mediterranean and Asian cuisine with a dash of Mexican. And same as their music, they often have culinary take over with guest chefs from acclaimed restaurants in the city.

Open: Sun - Tue 1pm - 12 am / Wed - Sat 1pm - 2am

Where: Juárez

Address: Toledo 39 (Go straight to the penthouse!)

@toledorooftop

....

XAMAN

Bar? Nightclub? A little bit of both. This underground bar is pumping to a soundtrack that will transport you all the way to an ecstatic dance session in Tulum or Bali. Lowlights, yurt-like booths, and a herbology-inspired menu that uses wild herbs and several peculiar ingredients. This place is usually filled with foreigners, and it's a good place to have a cocktail and…and a liberating tribal dance session.

Open: Tue - Sat 6pm - 2am

Where: Juárez

Address: Copenhague 6

@xamanbar

....

FIFTY MILS

So maybe you can't stay at the posh and dazzling Four Seasons, but you can come to their award-winning swanky bar Fifty Mils for a cocktail or two. The concept for Fifty mils (named after the fifty milliliters measure bartenders use) is more that of a mixology lab. Cocktails, both classic and new creations, are made with local ingredients and artisanal techniques. Come sit at their long and wide marble bar, and watch the shaker show put on by some of the best mixologists in all of Latin America. Plus…this is your chance to meet some rich hot international travelers at the bar. #NoShame

Open: Mon - Sat 5pm - 10pm

Where: Inside Four Seasons

Address: Paseo de la Reforma 500

@fiftymils

....

PARKER AND LENOX

Although it sounds like just one name, this place is actually two places in one. On the outside, Lenox, a snug diner-style restaurant rolling out high-end burgers and other snacks. But behind lies Parker, a quasi-speakeasy dedicated to live music, mostly jazz and blues, and full of sexy lounge areas scattered around the stage. If you didn't know Parker existed, you might think Lenox was all there was to this place. You can come to have a bite at the front and then head to Parker for some tunes, or head straight to Parker for a cocktail and order a bite from Lenox.

Open: Tue - Sat 6pm - 1am
Where: Juárez
Address: Calle Milán 14
@parkerandlenox

....

LE TACHINOMI DESU

Following this area's reputation of being home to many Japanese spots, Le Tachinomi Desu is a Japanese standing bar with Japanese whiskies and natural wines served at their sleek marble bartop. Although this place is pricier than other bars around the area, it's a very nice spot for a date or a special occasion…and probably the same prices you're used to back home. I love how tiny and squished together you get with people at the bar. That's how you make friends.

Open: Mon - Sat 7pm - 2am
Where: Cuauhtemoc
Address: Río Pánuco 132B
@letachinomidesu

MUCHO: MUSEO DEL CHOCOLATE

An unusual yet fun museum tucked away in an old house in La Juárez. The Chocolate Museum celebrates Cacao, which is native to Mexico, and takes you on a small tour of cacao's history. But it's not all data! They have some interactive sensory exhibits where you can smell and taste chocolate. And, of course, you'll walk out with the biggest craving for chocolate ever, so you can stop at the gift shop to buy some to take home (or devour right away), or stop at the cafe for some chocolate caliente. Ps. There are also chocolate-making workshops available.

Budget: $75 pesos
Open: Daily 11am - 5pm
Where: Juárez
Address: Milán 45

…and eat. Or get your visa at an embassy. That's it. Head into Roma for all the fun.

Shopping in Cuauhtemoc, Zona Rosa & Juarez

Mexican fashion, handcrafted home goods, alternative printshops, and all the vintage treasures you can find. Colonia Juarez has become the area to go shopping in Mexico City. Here's a quick guide to some of the

INCENDIARIAS

More than a shop, this is the physical headquarters of the feminist collective Mujeres Incendiarias, where they host talks and workshops. But they also sell fun, beautiful female-celebrating objects like tote bags, candles, and handcrafted boob-shaped mugs.

⊘ **Open:** Daily 11am-7:30pm
📍 **Address:** Marsella 60
@incendiarias__

....

FABRICA SOCIAL

Translating as Social Factory, this store is a platform to showcase the work of female artisans in Mexico and their knowledge of traditional weaving techniques. Here you can find the most beautiful, handcrafted clothes that you know for a fact are fair trade.

⊘ **Open:** Daily 11am - 7:30pm
📍 **Address:** Dinamarca 66
@fabricasocial

....

BAZAR FUSION

Start here. Bazar Fusion is best described as an upscale Mexican market with small shops selling high-quality handicrafts, jewelry, organic cotton PJs for kids, tea stores, bath products - everything. I love Bazar Fusion for the whimsical shopping experience but also because the products are all made with integrity!

⊘ **Open:** Tue- Sun 11am - 7pm
📍 **Address:** Londres 37
@bazarfusion

LOOSE BLUES

A vintage-inspired lifestyle shop full of brands from the U.S., Mexico, and Japan, this is one of those places that when you walk in, you can help but say "Man. Mexico City is cool...". Items here are high-quality and high-end, but they are true gems that any fashionista will appreciate. After you've shopped til you've dropped, head upstairs to the Dining Bar above the store, where they serve Japanese and Mexican fusion dishes paired with great jazz, funk, and blues.

⊙ **Open:** Mon 12pm - 8pm (shop only!) / Tue - Sat 12pm - 11pm / Sun 12pm - 7pm
🛏 **Address:** Dinamarca 44

@loose_blues

CAN CAN PROJECTS

Quirky and fun art prints and books that the people from Can Can Press call "underground souvenirs." Rightly so! This place feels very underground and urban cool. And hey, an art print is so easy to pack that it's the perfect thing to take back home.

⊙ **Open:** 11am - 7pm
🛏 **Address:** Marsella 56

@cancanpress

✎ **TRAVEL NOTES:**

....

....

....

....

....

....

Centro Historico

THE VIBE:

Europe with tacos

BEST FOR:

Diving deeper into the history and culture of Mexico City

while marveling at beautiful historic buildings

DAYS NEEDED:

One or two will suffice, but the more, the better!

Centro Historico

Technically speaking, Centro Historico is Mexico City's most touristic area...but it doesn't feel that way at all! That's the thing with Mexico, many touristic areas are also the space and stage where real and raw local life happens. And there are fewer more authentic areas in this country than Mexico City's downtown area.

Centro Historico has been the heart of the city for centuries. It was also the center of the ancient Aztec city of Tenochtitlan, founded around 1325. When the Spaniards arrived, they built on top of what already existed, keeping the urban design very much the same. So if there's an area where you can truly witness the rich layers of Mexico City's history and culture, it's here.

Until the 1800s, Centro Historico was all there was to Mexico City. Beyond this area was really nothing. Then the city started expanding, and people migrated to the new developing boroughs; Centro began booming as a hub for commerce and business life. This area also has been and continues to be the stage for celebrations and protests alike. That's the sign of a true centro.

But the Centro Historico is not just historic. It's artsy, it's academic, and it's even a little punk rock. It's a brewing pot of people from all kinds of backgrounds. Youngsters, government functionaries, businessmen, local vendors, and of course, tourists gazing at the beautiful buildings and touristic displays on the chaotic streets.

Centro Historico is definitely a must-stop on your Mexico City trip. It can be a bit chaotic but in a wonderful way. Hold my hand, and let me guide you through the crowds and away from the tourist traps. And straight to all the trendy spots and hidden gems.

WHAT ARE THESE?

Organilleros

When walking around Centro Historico, it's inevitable to see one of these guys playing a box-like instrument. They are street organ grinders (that's such a weird term, I know) delivering Mexican classics like "Cielito Lindo", and their slightly-out-of-tune, nostalgic sound has been part of the city's soundtrack for over a Century.

There are fewer and fewer Organillers on the streets as time goes by. It's a dying art, overrun by the colossal amount of street performers in Mexico City. But musicians still endure to keep this tradition alive. If you have a spare coin or two, make sure to donate to help keep this dying art from disappearing.

Areas to Know in Centro Historico

Don't be fooled. At first glance, the Centro Historico might look overwhelming with its tall buildings and busy pedestrians, but this area is pretty straightforward and easy to navigate! Especially because most points of reference are landmarks or big buildings. You can't screw this up. So here are just a few references for you to begin and end your exploration of Centro Historico...without spoiling all the fun that comes next in this chapter.

ALAMEDA CENTRAL

A public park that is the perfect spot to start your tour of downtown. Have your car drop you here, and then just walk around.

BELLAS ARTES

That beautiful all-white marble palace with a glass dome? That's Bellas Artes! We'll get to know it later in this chapter, but for now, it's the perfect guiding post as you explore this area.

LÁZARO CÁRDENAS EJE CENTRAL

Right after Bellas Artes, this big avenue crosses and marks the beginning of the most historic area. Right after you cross this avenue, you'll find yourself wandering narrower streets lined with colonial buildings.

FRANCISCO I. MADERO STREET

I'd recommend crossing Lázaro Cárdenas Eje Central into Ave. 5 de Mayo. It's a small street and a beautiful walk towards the Zocalo.

ZOCALO

The main plaza in Mexico City. A vast esplanade surrounded by colonial buildings and the Metropolitan Cathedral.

PALACIO NACIONAL

One of the colonial buildings that stand at the end of the Zocalo. These are a row of government buildings that houses Mexico's Federal Treasury and National Archives, spanning one entire side of the Zocalo square. This is also a good ending point to your history tour. You can now head back towards Alameda Central to make your way back.

Bring this book to life! Check out the mini video guides to Mexico City here on Alexa's IG highlight:

Where to Eat in Centro Historico

COFFEE, BREAKFAST & BRUNCH

CAFE DON PORFIRIO

Want your cappuccino with a side of the best view downtown? Cafe Don Porfirio is located just across the street from Bellas Artes...and on the top floor, so you get a full frontal magnificent view of this magnificent palace. To find this place, just walk into the Sears department store, head to the elevator, and hit level 8. And there you go. Coffee and breakfast with a view.

⊙ **Open:** Daily 11am - 8pm
♥ **Where:** Inside the Sears store, on the 8th floor
🏠 **Address:** Avenida Juárex 14

....

CAFE REGINA

Located on the Regina Corridor, a walking street that serves as a cultural passage is also one of the oldest streets in the city, Cafe Regina is exactly what you'd expect

a classic cafe in a big city to be: little tables on the sidewalk with historic buildings looming above. Lattes and sandwiches, eggs and pancakes, and croissants. Mostly locals flow in and out throughout the day, stopping to gossip with friends or to caffeinate before going to work. Come sit here with your treats, watch the people walk by, and get a real feel of life downtown.

⊙ **Open:** Mon, Tue, Wed 8am - 9 pm / Thu 8am - 12am / Fri - Sat 8am - 12 am / Sun 9am - 5pm
Where: Regina Corridor, Centro
🏠 **Address:** Calle Regina 24
@cafe_regina

....

PASTELERÍA IDEAL

Founded in 1927, Pastelería Ideal is a staple in the Mexico City breakfast world! You've never seen so many pastries in your life! Go there early enough in the mornings and watch the delivery drivers and interns filling to-go boxes with their day's worth of pastries. You, however, are going to have a more difficult time trying to choose just one or two treats - but hey, take an extra and keep it in your tote bag for later. Grab a tray and some tongs, and select your goodies. This place is super clean, by the way, so don't get weirded out by the tongs situation. Oh, and bring cash! They don't accept cards! When you're finished, meander upstairs and take a look at their collection of grandiose cakes made for Mexican weddings, birthdays, and quinceañeras!

⊙ **Open:** Daily 5am-8pm

♥ **Where:** 3.5 blocks southwest of Zócalo

🚇 **Address:** República de Uruguay 74

....

EL 123

This place goes from a French bistro in the mornings to a Thai eatery in the afternoon. Come for a Croque Monsieur in the morning and return for a green curry after you walk up an appetite. This cafe is housed within a shop and gallery called El Articulo 123, so don't forget to head upstairs when you're finished eating to peruse their current exhibit.

⊙ **Open:** Mon-Thu 12pm-7pm / Fri-Sun 12pm-8pm

♥ **Where:** Centro Historico

🚇 **Address:** Articulo 123

@articulo123mx

STREET FOOD & LOCAL SPOTS

CAFÉ DE TACUBA

This place is an institution, operating for over a century. Cafe de Tacuba is set in an old colonial building covered in handmade colonial tiles with stained-glass windows and brass details. It's a fairytale setting with traditional Mexican food like tamales and enchiladas and even Emy's favorite refreshing drink, agua de jamaica (try it here). For many, it's the epitome of the magical Mexican food experience. So much so, that Cafe de Tacuba has been a long-time favorite of Mexico's artists and literati. It's so iconic that it even originated the name of one of Mexico's most famous rock bands, Cafe Tacuba. Don't miss this spot.

⊙ **Open:** Daily 10am-10pm

♥ **Where:** Centro Historico

🚇 **Address:** Tacuba 28

TACOS LOS COCUYOS

Just a few blocks away from the Zocalo is this little gem. It's a must-stop when you're exploring downtown. Los Cocuyos is a tiny taqueria with only two guys inside doing the most in-sync dance of chopping, cooking, and serving that goes on for 24 hours. That's right, they're always open. These are tacos for the brave of mouth... they have everything: eyes, brains, cheek, head.

But if you're not feeling too adventurous, just go for the maciza (the leaner meats of pork) or the longaniza (delicious chorizo). Order a coke for the full Mexican street taco experience.

Ps. This place is beloved by locals and foreigners alike (even Anthony Bourdain visited back in the day). It can get crowded, but the line goes fast, and the tacos are worth the wait!

⊙ **Open:** 24 hours (seriously)
♀ **Where:** Centro Historico
🚂 **Address:** Bolívar 54

TACO DE LENGUA & LONGANIZA AT LOS COCUYOS

FUN FACT! Did you know Mexican Coca Cola is the only one in the world still made with natural, real sugar? That's why it's so strangely good and the best pairing for street tacos on a hot summer day.

MERCADO SAN JUAN

One of Mexico City's oldest markets and one of the most fascinating. Come here for an immersion into the most exotic corners of Mexican food. Deer, pheasant, squibs, alligators, iguana, rabbit, scorpions, and spiders are all available here for you to buy or try. You'll also find every unusual ingredient and spice you can imagine. I know, I know, this sounds like a dingy culinary black market, but it actually looks like a more sophisticated version of a traditional Mexican market. Besides the exotic bites, there are also more "normal" stalls selling Spanish cured ham and many other imported delicacies. This market is a chef's heaven.

⊙ **Open:** 7am - 6pm
♥ **Where:** Centro Historico
🏠 **Address:** 2° Calle de Ernesto Pugibet 21

LA RAMBLA

This spot is as local as it gets. It's so discreet that you'd likely miss it walking by (aren't ya glad you have this book!). La Rambla dates back to the early 1900s and has been known for decades for its tortas de Pavo (roast turkey tortas). This is a true working-class Mexican lunch. If you don't want to fill up on bread (tortas are quite filling), you can opt for turkey tacos! As usual with most local spots, this place is cash-only!

⊙ **Open:** Daily 8am - 10pm
♥ **Where:** Centro Historico (just a few blocks away from Bellas Artes)
🏠 **Address:** Motolinia 38

EL CARDENAL

Downtown Mexico City is full of tunnels back in time, and El Cardenal is surely one of them. It's a sophisticated Mexican restaurant where the tables are covered in white linens, and the servers are wearing formal attire - but the food is nothing but casual. Order the Mexican staples like chilaquiles verde con pollo or chiles rellenos. Or, if you like to start the day sweet, order the concha con nata (Mexican pastry with cream). To make this a real traditional Mexican breakfast experience, pair that with a chocolate caliente (hot chocolate).

⊙ **Open:** Daily 8am - 6:30pm
♥ **Where:** Centro Historico
🏠 **Address:** Calle de la Palma 23

LIMOSNEROS

Mexican classics with a modern makeover! The menu here focuses on seasonal ingredients and traditional cooking techniques, serving staple dishes like carnitas but made with rabbit instead of pork. The building, however, remains traditional. Limosneros takes its name after its walls, which are made with a collage of stones. When this building was originally built back in the late 1500s, they used an assortment of donated stones from other construction projects. This gave the walls the nickname of "paredes limosneros" - beggar walls.

Ps. Do not miss the buñuelo for dessert! And if you're in a drinking mood, here is a great place to sip on Pox and Sotol, another couple of traditional distilled-agave drinks that are usually overshadowed by Mezcal and Tequila.

Pss. Limosneros offers a 7-course tasting menu with a cocktail pairing which really highlights their culinary vision!

⊙ **Open:** Mon - Sat 1:30pm - 10 pm / Sun 1pm - 7pm
♥ **Where:** Centro Historico
🏠 **Address:** Allende 3
@limosnerosmx

AZUL HISTORICO

I'll be honest, this place wouldn't be my first choice for a solo traveler; but it's so beautiful and iconic we just couldn't leave it out! With a kitchen run by a food historian, Azul Historico is quintessential Mexico City, serving the most perfect versions of Mexican classics like mole negro and chipotle enchiladas...with the freshest tortillas made on site by the loveliest female tortilleras! Azul Historico is located in the beautiful courtyard of the Downtown Mexico Hotel, so you can expect the ambiance to be a little posh but still very casual. Save this place for a fancy solo date or to celebrate life with your new Mexico City friends.

⊙ **Open:** Daily 9am - 11pm
♥ **Where:** Downtown Mexico Hotel
🏠 **Address:** Isabel La Catolica 30
@azulhistorico

PIZZA...JUST IN CASE

CANCINO ALAMEDA

Once you've had your fill of Mexican snacks, then Cancino is here to save you with crispy, cheesy, wood-oven pizzas and craft beer and enjoy. The service is fast, the ambiance is chill and the food is fantastic. You might not think you'll want to eat pizza now, but pizza cravings follow me around the world...and they'll likely follow you, too. Now you know what to do when they hit. Ps. Cancino has different locations, so these pizzas will be within your reach even if you're in La Roma or Polanco.

⊙ **Open:** Daily 1pm-12am
♥ **Where:** Centro, inside the Barrio Alameda building
🛱 **Address:** Dr. Mora 9
@loscancinos

SWEETS & DESSERT

CHURRERIA EL MORO

The original churreria El Moro. This location is the one that opened back in 1935, after Don Francisco Iriarte, an immigrant from Spain, became known for selling churros in a cart around the Zocalo. And this place has not stopped selling churros ever since. Unlike the other locations that were rebranded a few years ago, this one keeps its original appearance. So you can forget about Instagrammers taking photos here; this one's packed with locals waiting to enjoy the delicious sugary crunch of freshly made churros.

⊙ **Open:** Daily 7am - 11pm
♥ **Where:** Centro Historico, a few blocks away from Bellas Artes
🛱 **Address:** Eje Central Lazaro Cardenas 42
@churreriaelmoro

Drinking Day & Night in Centro Historico

TERRAZA CATEDRAL

A bar for the guests of Hostel Mundo Joven Catedral

Traveling alone? Want to meet other travelers? This is the place to do it. This hostel bar is one of the most beautiful hidden gems in the city, with incredible glittering views of the Cathedral. I love the layout of this bar because it's designed to make meeting people easy! There's a bar top where you can sit, and plenty of bar tables scrunched close together. People are friendly and welcoming, don't be afraid to say hi to strangers or throw out an easy "Where ya from" to get the convo started.

BONUS: On Thursdays, they have Jazz music, and Fridays and Saturdays, they have a DJ with electronic music.

☉ **Open:** Daily - but access closes at 10pm

🛥 **Budget:** Only on Fridays and Saturdays do you need to pay an entry fee. $80 pesos on Friday and $100 pesos on Saturday.

♥ **Where:** Centro Historico

🚌 **Address:** República de Guatemala 4

⊕ **Make Reservations:** Thursdays, Fridays, and Saturdays at least three days in advance. To do this, send them a direct message:

🅵 facebook.com/terrazacatedralmx
✉ info@terrazacatedral.com.

....

ZINCO JAZZ BAR

Jazz lovers, rejoice! This is where all the great music is at. All the major jazz acts that come to Mexico City come straight here, so there's always something good on the roster. And even if you're not that big of a fan of jazz, the place is amazing. It's housed in the former vaults of an Art Deco bank building, so walking in it feels like a Gatsby-esque speakeasy adventure.

☉ **Open:** Mon - Sat 10am - 6pm
♥ **Where:** Centro Historico
🚌 **Address:** Motolinia 20
@zincojazzbar

BOSFORO

A mezcaleria so dimly lit and mysterious, walking into Bosforo will make you feel like you're in a spy movie on assignment somewhere exotic. Except in real life, no one will chase you, instead, you'll be chasing sips of mezcal with roasted peanuts and crispy grasshoppers. Bosforo serves various mezcal from all over the country and plays funky tunes curated by the owner himself. This place is as hip and hipster as it can be. And it's tiny, so if you're planning to come during the weekend, come early.

⊘ **Open:** Tue-Wed 6pm - 1:30am / Thu-Sat 6pm - 2:30am
Where: Centro Historico
Address: Luis Moya 31

COFFEE SHOP 42

Pulque. You've likely never tried this historic drink called the "drink of the gods" by the Aztecs...and you should try it before you go! Pulque is made by fermenting the sap from an agave plant, and it's a bit...slimy. Some people love it, some people are fine with just trying it for cultural purposes and then moving on to a mezcal cocktail. Coffee Shop 42 has the pulque and also has kind of a Thailand vibe to it with trippy lighting and neon colors. It's a vibe. And hey, if you end up liking this place, come back for coffee to fix your hangover in the AM.

⊘ **Open:** Mon - Sat 10am - 6pm
Where: Centro Historico
Address: Motolinia 20

DOWNTOWN MEXICO HOTEL TERRACE

The rooftop bar at this hotel is the place to go for views! City views and people-watching views. I mean, have you ever gone to a hotel bar before? It's full of fascinating travelers (some of which are single, wink wink). Downtown Mexico has incredible cocktails and food but officially requires a reservation if you're not staying there. To get to the terrace, take the elevator by the main entrance of the hotel. Press "T" for the terrace.

⊘ **Open:** 10:30am - 12am
Where: Centro Historico
Address: Isabel la Catolica 30
Book via Whatsapp: +52 155 5280 1813

Things to Do & See in Centro Historico

HISTORY HOP

Below is a list of every worth-it historical sight to see in Centro Historico, but where do you start?

To make things easy for you, we've numbered the places in the order we'd recommend you visit them, and we'll dive into each of these in the next few pages.

1. ALAMEDA CENTRAL
2. BELLAS ARTES
3. PALACIO POSTAL
4. TORRE LATINOAMERICANA
5. CASA DE LOS AZULEJOS
6. EL ZOCALO
7. CATEDRAL METROPOLITANA
8. PALACIO NACIONAL
9. TEMPLO MAYOR
10. GRAN HOTEL

And to make it even easier, just can this code to access your Mexico City map and find the "History Hop" section ☞

Have your Uber drop you at Alameda Central, a public park that happens to be the oldest park in the American continent...and a former marketplace for the Aztecs! This esplanade is the perfect spot to start your tour of downtown. When you're ready to leave this area, you can use this same spot to get an Uber to pick you up.

Ps. Feel free to skip what you want.

PALACIO DE BELLAS ARTES (PALACE OF FINE ARTS)

Opulent and elegant, this beautiful white-marble palace that you'll see right on the Alameda Central is one of the main attractions of the city. Bellas Artes, the Palace of Fine Arts in English, is the epitome of the art and culture of Mexico City. It's entirely built of Carrara marble and is known for its murals by Diego Rivera, Siqueiros, and other iconic painters of the early 1900s.

It's home to the Bellas Artes Palace Museum, the National Museum of Architecture, and the National Theater (a world–renowned opera house). Bellas Artes has been the venue and stage for many historical events as well as international opera, dance, music, art, and literature.

Bellas Artes was started in 1905 but wasn't finished until 1934 because the Revolutionary War happened in between. It took so much time to build it that it's made in two totally different styles. The inside is completely Art Nouveau, but by the time they got to the interiors, Art Deco was in full rage. But beyond these art styles, you can see a lot of Aztec-inspired motifs if you look closely.

Bellas Artes often has pretty cool temporary exhibitions, so check beforehand what's on the roster on their website. Visit: ⊕ museopalaciodebellasartes.gob.mx to check their calendar.

🏷 **Budget:** $80 pesos entrance fee
◎ **Open:** Tue-Sun 11am - 5pm / Closed on Mondays
🚇 **Address:** Eje Lazaro Cardenas S/N

FUN FACT! Bellas Artes is sinking. Since Mexico City was built on not very solid ground, this building is so heavy that it sinks about 2 inches every year!

DISCOVER THE PALACIO POSTAL

This spot is a true hidden gem. Not visited by many but one of my favorite stops downtown. On the outside, this building is built completely with limestone, but it's the inside that will completely blow you away. I don't want to give too much away, so trust me that it's a must-visit. And yes, this is still an operating postal office. Kinda makes you wish that all postal offices were still like this, right?

◎ **Open:** Mon-Fri 8am - 8pm / Sat 9am - 15pm
♀ **Where:** Centro Historico (across the street from Bellas Artes
🚇 **Address:** Tacuba 1

FUN FACT! When this building was inaugurated in 1907, it was Frida Kahlo's father, Guillermo Kahlo, who created the illustrations for the newspaper. You can still see this 100-year-old paper framed and hanging at the palace's entrance.

WATCH THE VIEW FROM THE TOP OF THE TORRE LATINO

Do you want to see the city from 44 stories high? The Torre Latinoamericana is another one of Mexico City's most-known landmarks. Not only for its facade but for the grandiose view it offers and the opportunity to truly grasp how big this city is. However, as cool as the view is, I must warn you that this place gets crowded and some waiting might be involved.

However, pro tip…if you ask the doorman for the bar, you'll be directed to a separate elevator away from the crowds. You'll have to buy a beer, but hey, best beer money ever spent. This tower was one of the first skyscrapers in the city, and it was the first skyscraper to be ever successfully built in a seismic area. Impressive right?

🎟 **Budget:** $7 USD ($125 pesos)
⊙ **Open:** Daily 9am - 10pm
🏛 **Address:** Eje Central Lázaro Cárdenas

LA CASA DE LOS AZULEJOS

One of the most beautiful buildings in all of Mexico City. This place is called "The House of Tiles" because it's completely covered in blue and white Talavera (traditional hand-painted ceramic) tiles. It's quite a sight from the outside but also the inside. Walk in and marvel at the moldings, the ceilings and, the general splendor. The building houses a restaurant and a department store called Sanborns. The restaurant is widely famous for its enchiladas, and the store is… just a nice air-conditioned pit-stop in your day of exploring. Pro Tip! This is the perfect spot for a (clean and bougie) bathroom stop if you're walking around the area. Make sure you have a $5 peso coin with you for this!

EL ZOCALO

The main plaza in Mexico City is called El Zocalo. Here is where life begins and ends; it's the center of the universe in Centro Historico. If you look around, you'll find yourself surrounded by colonial buildings. But underneath, below the heavy Cantera and herds of people and tourists, lay the remains of Tenochtitlan, the capital of the Aztec empire. When the Spanish came, they built their empire literally on top of what already existed. This is where you can see, live and breathe how this city is built and formed by layers. Besides the Aztec remains, el Zocalo has been the stage for many historical events, from protests to concerts. Look up and take it all in: you're standing in the very heart of Mexico. Ps. I adore this area at night. It lights up like a Disney movie.

CATEDRAL METROPOLITANA

A Roman Catholic church situated atop a sacred Aztec precinct. Its construction began right after the Spanish conquest happened, and it was originally designed after the Gothic cathedrals in Spain, but its construction took around 250 years, so it ended up being a patchwork of architectural styles. This Cathedral is a big part of Mexico's cultural identity, and thousands of legitimate devotees (rather than just tourists) visit it daily. You can walk it and admire the baroque interiors, but if there's a service in progress, don't forget to be respectful!

🏷 **Budget:** Free
⊙ **Open:** Mon - Sun 8am - 8pm
🏛 **Address:** Pza. de la Constitución S/N

LOCAL PRO TIP!

If you have time and are a fan of history and architecture and, well, churches, visit the San Francisco church. Just a few blocks away from Bellas Artes, this is the oldest and most beautiful church in Mexico City, according to Emy's grandma. Grandma Vicky was born and raised in the city and came to this very church with her mother every Sunday. She says the hand-carved stone facade and the wall-sized altar covered in gold leaf are worth admiring. Find it at Ave. Francisco I. Madero 7.

PALACIO NACIONAL

This colonial building houses the greatest Diego Rivera murals and many other art pieces portraying passages of Mexico's history. Palacio Nacional is not just a historic palace, it's governmental offices, and you'll bump elbows with functionaries and government officials here. This is a great spot to learn about Mexico's history…and it's present.

🏷 **Budget:** Free
⊙ **Open:** Tue-Sun 10am-5pm
🏛 **Address:** Plaza de la Constitución S/N

TEMPLO MAYOR

Just to the Cathedral's right, you will find the Museo del Templo Mayor, the archeological site where all the Aztec ruins sit. It functions as a museum where you can come and stare at history in the face. You can wander the structures and see ancient objects and artifacts displayed. The museum is a bit wider than it looks at first sight but still fairly easy to navigate and comprehend.

 Budget: $80 pesos
 Open: Tue, Wed, Fri, Sat, Sun 9am-5pm
 Address: Seminario 8

THE GRAN HOTEL

Insta spot alert! A former department store turned into a hotel with the most gorgeous Tiffany's stain-glass vault ceilings that will make you feel like you're in an old, glamorous movie. On the rooftop, there's a bar called La Terraza with one of the best views of the Zocalo. It's the perfect spot for a cocktail at sunset after a long day of exploring and walking around. This is a functioning hotel, by the way. So, if you're not planning to head up to La Terraza, just play it cool when you walk into the lobby. Pretend you stay there or something.

 Open: Mon-Fri 8am - 8pm / Sat 9am - 15pm
 Address: 16 de Septiembre 82

Museums to Visit in Centro Historico

MUSEO DE ARTE POPULAR

This museum is all about popular art in Mexico: crafts, everyday items, toys, garments…everything that makes Mexico such a colorful country. There's even a small section dedicated to the Day of the Dead. Unlike the Anthropological Museum, this one is a short and sweet visit. So if you don't have as much time in the city, this is a great way to take an express dive into Mexican culture.

🏷 **Budget:** $60 pesos / free for students, even international ones
⊙ **Open:** Tue-Sun 10am-6pm
🏛 **Address:** Revillagigedo 11

MUSEO FRANZ MAYER

This museum was built to hold the private collection of German businessman, Franz Mayer, which happens to be some of the most important decorative arts collections in all of Mexico. Emy claims this is the museum where she's seen some of the coolest art exhibits in the city. The building is also full of history, and its library is also open to the public. It holds over 14,000 volumes of antique and rare books and documents.

🏷 **Budget:** $75 pesos / free on Tuesdays
⊙ **Open:** Tue-Fri 10am - 5pm / Sat - Sun 11am - 6pm
🏛 **Address:** Hidalgo 45
@museofranzmayer

MUSEO DE MEMORIA & TOLERANCIA

This museum has nothing to do with Mexico, but it's quite an impressive experience. Named "The Memory and Tolerance Museum", this museum is divided into two sections. The first part, Memory, travels back in time to the Holocaust and through other crimes against humanity, like the Rwanda genocide. The second part, Tolerance, focuses on solutions and hope. It addresses dialogues, human rights, and the power of the media as an advocate for diversity. This museum works under the premise that remembering history will help us prevent repeating it, and the experience will definitely bring you to ask yourself questions about how we can live with more empathy and sensibility.

🎟 **Budget:** $105 pesos
🕙 **Open:** Tue-Sun 10am-6pm
🏛 **Address:** Av. Juárez 8
@memoriaytolerancia

MUSEO DE ARTE NACIONAL (MUNAL)

The Museum of National Art portrays the history of Mexican Fine Arts with pieces from the colonial period to contemporary photography. This museum is great if you want to dive deeper into Mexican history and culture and go way beyond the image the world has of Mexico. Wander into the interior of the museum, which is pure splendor. Ornamented walls, and ceilings covered in murals, you'll wonder if you've somehow teleported to Europe.

🎟 **Budget:** $62 pesos
🕙 **Open:** Tue - Sun 11am - 5 pm
🏛 **Address:** Tacuba 8
@munalmx

Overwhelmed? Go on a museum tour with a guide:

Other Things to Do in Centro Historico

ATTEND A LUCHA LIBRE MATCH AT ARENA COLISEO

It's a cultural must and a fun way to spend Saturday evenings. Refer to the section in the Top 7 Things You Must Do in Mexico City on page 96.

DAY PASS AT DOWNTOWN MEXICO HOTEL'S TERRACE POOL

The restaurant from above has a pool and a day pass! The day pass for the pool costs $600 pesos and includes 2 non-alcoholic drinks and an entree. In the warmer months (end of April to early June), the pool is a fun way to spend a relaxing day. Go sightseeing in the morning, and then come here when the sun is highest in the sky for lunch and a couple of drinks in your suit.

🏠 **Address:** Isabel la Catolica 30
Book via Whatsapp: +52 155 5280 1813

WATCH A FILM AT LA CASA DEL CINE

La Casa del Cine is an art-cinema house that showcases independent films from all over the world and from Mexican creators too. It's a small space with two projection rooms and a roster of 3 movies a week. If you're a cinephile, you'll absolutely love this place. And not just for the movies. The space is really cool, housed within an old colonial hidden behind a bright red door.

✒ **Budget:** $66 pesos, but they often have free screenings as well
☉ **Open:** Tue - Sat 1pm - 11pm / Sun 1pm - 8pm
🏠 **Address:** República de Uruguay 52
@lacasadelcinemx

LISTEN TO MARIACHI AT PLAZA GARIBALDI

The iconic Plaza Garibaldi is an outdoor plaza that's kind of the mothership for Mariachis. You can come during the day or at night for this traditional Mexican experience. The plaza is surrounded by cantinas and bars, but I recommend hitting the Salón Tenampa for a drink while you listen to the songs other patrons have requested. Dinner time is high-time for Mariachis. Ps. I wouldn't recommend coming alone at night!

⊙ **Open:** Daily 1pm-12am
🏛 **Address:** Eje Central Lázaro Cárdenas 43

DID YOU KNOW? ━━━━━━━━━━━━━━━━

Mariachi is a genre of regional Mexican music. They're originally from the state of Jalisco, but Mariachi bands have become an icon of Mexican culture. They usually consist of as many as eight violins, two trumpets, one guitar, a vihuela, a guitarron (acoustic bass), with vocals being sung by different members depending on the song. They are distinguished by their "Charro" costume, a black, white or burgundy suit with silver embellishments. And of course, the round, embroidered hat!

VISIT THE VASCONCELOS LIBRARY

Though this library is a failed governmental project, it is mostly famous for its unbelievable architecture. When you walk in, you're faced with a system of suspended, expandable shelves that feels like a scene from a sci-fi movie. This is a stop for architecture buffs; if that's not you, I wouldn't make it a priority.

🏷 **Budget:** Free
⊙ **Open:** Daily 8:30am - 7:30pm
🚇 **Address:** Eje 1 Norte Mosqueta S/N

EXPLORE EL BARRIO CHINO, MEXICO CITY'S CHINATOWN

As to be expected in a big metropolis, there's a Chinatown in Mexico City! The Mexican Barrio Chino isn't very well-known or famous, and it's sprawled over just two blocks which consists mostly of Chinese eateries and shops stocked with imported goods. Plus, there's a live market on Sundays. But...I don't usually recommend this area to my friends. It's not as alive as the rest of the city and not even as alive as the Chinatowns you're used to visiting around the globe.

🚇 **Address:** Dolores S/N

SHOPPING IN CENTRO HISTORICO
LA CIUDADELA MARKET

A market exclusively for arts and crafts. Aisles and aisles stuffed with ceramics from Puebla, textiles from Oaxaca, figurines from Nayarit... every kind of Mexican craft from all the different corners of the country. This market is a visual journey of colors and textures. And if you want to take souvenirs home, this is the place to get them. Don't forget to bring cash, and yes, it's acceptable to barter a little!

⊙ **Open:** Mon-Sat 10am-7pm / Sun 10am-6pm
🚇 **Address:** Balderas S/N

CHAPTER SIX

Polanco

●━━━━━●

THE VIBE:

Posh and swanky, but still a bit residential
and charming during the day

BEST FOR:

Fine-dining, boozy brunches and great shopping

DAYS NEEDED:

Just one

●━━━━━●

CHAPTER SIX

Polanco

Polanco, often called Mexico City's "Beverly Hills," is where glitz and glamor hang out; a destination for fine-dining, snazzy cocktails, and some serious shopping. It is the playground for the rich and famous and the wanna-be-rich and famous too. And that's the thing I don't particularly love: it sometimes feels like a stage for posing and pretending.

But it's not all showoffs in Polanco, and it's not all splurging and drinking. This area still holds a residential and charming feel to it. With its classic, European-style old mansions and medians lined with bright flowers, it's a lovely area to dive deeper into this layer of Mexico, visit some incredible museums, and sit on a sunny terrace with a cup of coffee…or an Aperol Spritz. It's also home to some of the best fine-dining restaurants in the world. Yes, in the world!

How did Polanco get like this? Originally, Polanco was a residential area and home of the upper class that fled other neighborhoods like La Roma, so it started off as a place of affluence right away. But it wasn't all about class and wealth back then, you'll notice all streets are named after writers, philosophers, and poets like Jules Verne and Edgar Allan Poe. This area celebrated academia, culture, and education. With time though, it's become more about status and the labels than culture, turning it into the swanky, flashy neighborhood it is today.

But I'll be honest, Polanco is not my top-rated area in Mexico City. It's fancy and safe, but it's not as culturally exciting or raw as the other areas in this book. And so, I recommend you plan to interact with Polanco in one of two ways

→ **Option 1:** Stay here at one of my favorite hotels, Pugseal. You'll use this as your ultra-comfortable hub. You'll wander into other neighborhoods during the day and return to Polanco after the sun comes down. You'll eat a couple of really great meals here.

→ **Option 2:** You will stay in a more affordable area like Roma Norte and visit Polanco on a food and drink mission one evening - that's all.

Areas to Know in Polanco

Polanco is the name for quite an extensive area that is divided into 5 different sections, but most things to do in Polanco are in the same area. So to avoid confusion, we're skipping those 5 sections and referring to Polanco as a whole. Trust me, that's extra information your travel brain won't need. All you need to know are these three important points in Polanco that will help you navigate through the neighborhood.

AVENIDA MASARYK

Mexico's 5th Avenue...but even bougier. Avenida Masaryk is Polanco's main drag lined with Gucci, Hermes, Dolce & Gabbana, and more luxury stores I can't afford. This avenue is so over the top that the sidewalks are paved with marble. Yep, real marble. If you ever thought Mexico was all cobblestones and cacti, now you know Polanco.

PARQUE LINCOLN

Yep, you're in Polanco, so naturally, this is the city's most manicured park. It runs along Emilio Castelar, conveniently facing many cafes and restaurants. And in case you were wondering about the name, Parque Lincoln is indeed named after Abraham Lincoln because he openly opposed the American-Mexican war of 1846, winning the hearts of Mexicans.

POLANQUITO

Polanquito is the heart of Polanco. It's a small area located along Lincoln Park, consisting of just a few streets, but it's where the most popular restaurants, cafes, and many luxury shops are.

✎ **TRAVEL NOTES:**

Where to Eat in Polanco

COFFEE & COWORKING

CIELITO QUERIDO CAFE

This is Mexico's version of Starbucks, replacing the deep green and homey aesthetics for an explosion of color with a hint of irreverence. Their brand is all about bright graphics inspired by vintage Mexican signage, using fun proverbs and everyday phrases. When this chain opened about 10 years ago, it even made fun of Starbucks: their cups read: "it's called Large, not Venti…" and so on. But these days, they've opted for a sweeter tone that celebrates Mexican culture and spirit through their snacks and beverages. You can order a regular coffee, but you can also take advantage of the fact that you're in México and order a Café de Olla (sweet coffee brewed with sugar cane and cinnamon) to sip while you spend some time with your laptop.

⊙ **Open:** Mon - Fri 6am - 10pm / Sat 8am - 8pm / Sun 9am - 9pm
♀ **Where:** Polanco
🏠 **Address:** Homero 109
@cielitoqueridooficial

SESEN ROOM

Wellness women, get your highlighter ready because this one is for you! Sensen Room is the showroom for a brand with the same name, Sesen, that specializes in collagen and wellness supplements. But it's also a unique "collagen coffee bar" where they serve drinks like smoothies, cold pressed juice, tea, and coffee, all of which include collagen! So they're not only delicious, but they're extra healthy for you! Besides, the place is beautiful, with a sleek and clean aesthetic that is a Pinterest dream come true.

Ps. Sesen is female run and founded. This city is full of girl power!

⊙ **Open:** Mon - Fri 8am - 8pm / Sat - Sun 10am - 6pm
♀ **Where:** A few blocks away from Antara Fashion Hall
🏠 **Address:** Ave. Homero 1433
@sesenroom

BREAKFAST & BRUNCH

IVOIRE

Where Paris meets Polanco, according to their Instagram bio. Come to Ivoire for mimosas and start the day slowly! Ask to sit outside at their round tables lined up on the sidewalk, in true Parisian style, with a view of Lincoln Park. Expect to be surrounded by posh people drinking Aperol Spritz and eating escargot. The escargot is the thing to order here.

Ps. They recently remodeled their upstairs terrace and transformed it into Dirty Dandy, a sexy space with a fashionable crowd and a prime spot to grab a cocktail at night.

⊙ **Open:** Mon - Tue 8am - 12am / Wed 8am - 1am / Thu - Sat 8am - 2am / Sun 8am - 10pm
♀ **Where:** Polanquito, right across from Parque Lincoln
📍 **Address:** Emilio Castelar 95
@ivoiremx

MAQUE

This cute breakfast spot is a traditional Mexican pasteleria aka bakery. It's been beloved by locals for its cakes and pan dulce (Mexican pastries) since 1987. And beloved by Emy because of its conchas! They're perfectly sweet and fluffy! So if you want to try this iconic Mexican bread, do it here.

And if you want the full experience, order it "with nata", clotted cream that is sometimes used to accompany pastries both in Mexico and Spain. Ps. They have another location in Condesa right across Parque México, which is a great spot too.

⊙ **Open:** Mon - Sat 8am - 9pm / Sun 8am - 8pm
♀ **Where:** Polanquito
📍 **Address:** Emilio Castelar 209 G
@maquecafe

STREET FOOD & LOCAL SPOTS

SIEMBRA TORTILLERÍA

There are 59 varieties of corn in Mexico, but everyday tortillas are made with regular white GMO corn. That sucks, right? Thankfully, in the past few years, many projects have surfaced trying to rescue authentic maiz criollo and make it accessible again. One of these projects is Siembra Tortilleria. Tucked deep in the streets of Polanco, this tiny tortilleria focuses on fresh tortillas made with different kinds of authentic maiz. You can even buy masa to prepare tortillas back home. But if making tortillas sounds too daunting, eat here and try some snacks like tamales, tiny tlacoyos, or their taco of the day.

⊙ **Open:** Mon - Sat 7am - 6pm / Sun 8am - 4pm
♀ **Where:** Polanco
🏠 **Address:** Isaac Newton 256
@siembra.tortilleria

There's a popular saying in Mexico: "No hay país sin maíz" which translates to "there's no country without corn".

This is not Siembra Tortilleria, but this seems like a good moment to show you what a tortilla-making machine looks like. And to tell you that tortillerias are such an integral part to the daily life of Mexicans. People get their fresh tortillas daily from these little shops. You'll see tortillerias everywhere you go in Mexico and you'll even recognize their distinctive high-pitched grinding sound from afar.

And talking about sounds, here's a fun little journey through the sounds of Mexico City. Enjoy!

LA CASA DEL PASTOR

Street tacos gone a little fancy! But just a little bit. La Casa del Pastor is a simple taco stand that doesn't overcomplicate things. It does pastor tacos, and it does pastor tacos well! La Casa del Pastor is a boutique chain of taco stands which means they aren't the local-with-a-food- cart kind of place.

If you've been worried about eating street food, but you want to try street food, this place will suit you. Plus, the tacos are goooood that if I closed my eyes, I'd think I was eating them from a little cart in the most local of neighborhoods.

⊙ **Open:** Sun - Wed 8am - 12am / 8am - 4am
♥ **Where:** Polanco
🏠 **Address:** Alfredo Musset 3
@lacasadelpastor

TAQUERIA EL TURIX

This place will make you forget you're in bougie Polanco for a moment. El Turix stands as a monument to Polanco's older days before all the fritz and glam and designer stores took over the area. The menu here is simple: juicy cochinita pibil tacos, which is Yucatán-style slow-cooked spiced pork. These tacos are worth the trip to Polanco alone. Top your taco with pickled onion, and expect your taco to fall apart. They're just so juicy.

⊙ **Open:** Daily 10am - 10pm
♥ **Where:** Polanco
🏠 **Address:** Emilio Castelar 212

LUNCH & DINNER

PUJOL

So if you want the dining experience in the city, this is it. Featured on Netflix's Chef's Table Episode 4, Season 2 - this is the best of the best when it comes to fine dining in Mexico City.

Pujol reinvented fine dining and blew the culinary world wide open when chef Enrique Olvera took the taco from the streets and put it on a fine-dining plate. His food recovered ingredients and techniques in Mexican cuisine that had long been forgotten or taken for granted and changed the landscape of gastronomy in the country, putting Mexico on the fine-dining map. And so began the evolution of Mexico City into the culinary destination it is today. At Pujol, you can order a la carte, but I recommend you go all out with a tasting menu or the taco omakase. If you can, do not leave without trying their Mole Madre, a plate that consists of mole and mole alone. A spoonful of aged mole with a spoonful of fresh, new mole on top. Only a place this good could get away with serving a spoonful of sauce...and it becoming their superstar dish.

PRO TIP! Book way ahead. Pujol tends to be booked 2-3 months in advance.

⊙ **Open:** Mon - Sat 1pm - 10pm
♥ **Where:** Polanco
🏛 **Address:** Tennyson 133
@pujol

....

QUINTONIL

Like Pujol, Quintonil is also listed in the World's 50 Best lists. Even though it's not as high-ranked as Pujol, some say it's even better. Maybe it's because Quintonil is a little less sought after, and so the restaurant can afford to offer an experience that feels a bit more personal. Quintonil goes beyond the plate and its entire essence circles around the idea of cooking as an agent of change. You can order a la carte, or if you want to go full out, you can do the 10-course tasting menu (which I so recommend). The menu is very vegetable oriented, an ode to agriculture, no doubt, and it's constantly changing. The restaurant is never associated with any particular dish, making every visit a delicious and delightful surprise. As long as 10 courses may sound, it still is an intimate and personal experience. Ps. Book your table as far in advance as you can!

⊙ **Open:** Mon - Saturday 1pm - 5pm / 6:30pm - 10:30pm
♀ **Where:** Polanco
🏠 **Address:** Newton 55
@rest_quintonil

....

BLANCO CASTELAR

A Polanco institution, Blanco Castelar is most definitely one of the best restaurants in Polanco. Their menu is pretty extensive, and its contents are a bit of a mix. You'll find both sashimi and suckling pig tacos. As wide as the variety of dishes is, with hints of Mexican, European and Asian, the menu somehow makes perfect sense. Dinner here is always a good idea, and it's the kind of place where instead of an entree, you should go with a few appetizers so you can try more deliciousness.

Blanco Castelar is not just one of the best restaurants in town but one of the prettiest. An old mansion from the 1930s with chandeliers and all-black and white decor, this place feels like it could be the set of an Audrey Hepburn movie.

⊙ **Open:** Mon - Wed 1pm - 11pm / Thu - Sat 1pm - 2am / Sun 1pm - 6pm
♀ **Where:** Polanquito
🏠 **Address:** Emilia Castelar 163

CASA OLYMPIA

Cocktails...but make it Wes Anderson. With soft pastel colors and a minimalistic yet kitsch decor, Casa Olympia is #InstaGoals. But while visuals feed the soul, you're here to feed your belly. And feed it you will because food is great...and cocktails are even better. When you arrive, this place greets you with their house drink, the Olympia Spritz: a gin and prosecco cocktail with violet liqueur and flowers. Their menu is mostly Mediterranean food but with some quirky touches (like their Souvlaki Burger!). You'll fall in love both with the place and the plates at Casa Olympia.

⊙ **Open:** Wed - Thu 2pm - 2am / Fri - Sun 9am - 2am
♀ **Where:** Polanco
🏠 **Address:** Anatole France 70
@casa_olympia

....

TORI TORI

As funny as it sounds, Japanese food in Mexico is widely known for being amazing. And Tori Tori is one of the best of the best and a most beloved sushi spots for Mexico City residents. This top-notch sushi place has been around since the 90s and the menu spawns from traditional and true-to-its-origin japanese makis, to other more non-traditional rolls and dishes. Come here to take a break from Mexican flavors and treat yourself to a superb Japanese dinner. The prices are a bit elevated, so I would save this for a special occasion.

NOTE: There are two locations in Polanco, but I recommend the one in Anatole France because it's a cozier and has more of an intimate atmosphere, perfect for a solo date with some incredible sushi. The other location, however, has snazzy and avant-garde architecture that has become quite the insta-spot. If you're going with a party go to this second location on Temostocles street.

⊙ **Open:** Mon - Yue 1pm - 11pm / Wed 1pm - 12am / Thu-Sat 1pm-1am / Sun 1pm - 8pm
♀ **Where:** Both locations are a near Lincoln Park
🛕 **Address:**

♀ **Intimate location:** Anatole France 71B

♀ **Snazzy location:** Temistocles 61 @toritorimx

DUMAS MARKET

A self-proclaimed urban oasis, Dumas market is truly a break from all the bouginess of Polanco. Don't get me wrong, this is still a bougie and gourmet food market, but here you will find more casual but diverse bites like tapas and even some Indonesian dishes in a relaxed backyard-like setting. This place is great to come for a quick snack and a craft beer before you resume your Mexico City adventures.

⊙ **Open:** Mon - Sat 9am - 8pm / Sun 9am - 7pm
♀ **Where:** Almost on the corner of Masaryk Avenye and Alejandro Dumas
🛕 **Address:** Alejandro 125 @marche.dumas

Drinking Day & Night in Polanco

TICUCHI

A dimly-lit tavern-like bar that is another one of chef Enrique Olvera's babies throughout the city. But at Ticuchi, drinks take center stage while food consists of simple Mexican snacks to accompany the agave-focused spirits. Come here not only for mezcal but to try other Mexican distillates like Sotol and Bacanora. The menu is short and mostly vegetarian, with Olvera's signature use of Mexican ingredients like, of course, insects.

VERY RANDOM FUN FACT!
Ticuchi means "bat" in Toltec, an indigenous tongue. The name of this bar is inspired by the fact that long-nosed bats are essential in the pollination of agaves.

⊙ **Open:** Daily 6:30pm - 11:30pm
♥ **Where:** Polanco
🏛 **Address:** Petrarca 254
@ticuchi.mx

LICORERIA LIMANTOUR

Limantour is one of the top places in the city to go for a drink. And not just according to me: it is ranked N° 6 in the list of the World's 50 Best Bars. Needless to say, when it comes to cocktails, it is an institution.

Every season they have a new "chapter," a temporary menu with drinks designed by renowned mixologists around the world. Their current chapter, titled Confabulario, celebrates creativity and adds a few ounces of irreverence to the seriousness of Limantour. Their permanent menu has some must-try Mexican versions of classic drinks, like the Pastor Margarita. Intrigued to try? I was, too, and it was worth it!

⊙ **Open:** Mon 5pm - 12am / Tue 5pm - 2am / Wed - Fri 4pm - 2am / Sat 3pm - 2am / Sun 3pm - 2am
♥ **Where:** Polanco
🏛 **Address:** Oscar Wilde 9
@limantourmx

PUBBELLY

If you're looking for a trendy place to have a drink, come to Pubbelly. This place was first opened in Miami, and it's got all the Latin vibes going on, even though it's a sushi place...or something like that. It's a total mix of Latin and Asian ingredients, resulting in menu items like the Sushi Taquitos, but also items that are as made for the 'gram as they are for eating, like the chocolate gold cake.

The place is fun and vibrant, modeled after a food market, with long bars where you can sit and watch the chefs slice enormous tunas and turn them into delicious rolls.

⊘ **Open:** Mon - Tue 1pm - 12am / Wed - Sat 1pm - 2am / Sun 1pm - 11pm
♥ **Where:** Polanco
🛱 **Address:** Masaryk 275
@pubbellymasaryk

EL DEPOSITO WORLD BEER STORE

If you want to hit Polanco but fancy-schmancy cocktails aren't your thing, head to El Deposito. This place is a literal "deposito" (warehouse) where you can go on a *tour de monde* through artisanal beers. From Mexican Mezcal Pale Ales to Californian IPAs, and lots of special edition beers made through collaborations by local breweries, this place is craft beer heaven.

The space is a mix between a prohibition-era-inspired joint and a sports bar, serving beer-friendly snacks like wings and burgers. Ps. If you're a craft beer fiend like me, you'll be happy to know they have many locations across the city.

⊘ **Open:** Mon - Fri 1pm-1am
♥ **Where:** Polanco (20 min. Walk from Parque Lincoln)
🛱 **Address:** Av. Ejercito Nacional 468
@eldepositowbs

Things to Do in Polanco

STROLL ALONG PARQUE LINCOLN

Take a stroll along the park and take in Polanco's peaceful vibes. Parque Lincoln is also known as "Parque de Los Espejos" (Park of Mirrors) because it's full of ponds...and kids driving remote-controlled sailboats. The park is full of landmarks like the Clock Towers, the Abraham Lincoln aviary full of endemic and exotic birds, and the Angela Peralta open-air theater, where sometimes you catch some live jazz as well as sculptures and statues dispersed along the park. It runs along Emilio Castelar and faces many cafes and restaurants, so it's easy to take a stroll in the park after brunch.

MUSEO SOUMAYA

This museum has become more famous for its shiny, loud exterior than for the art it holds inside. An Instagram backdrop for visitors that has positioned the museum as a Mexico City landmark. In my opinion, this museum isn't worth all the rage. Sure, it holds treasures like Rodin and Salvador Dali sculpture replicas, but they're so crammed with other pieces you can't even appreciate them that well. If you have a short time in Mexico City choose your museums wisely and skip this one. However, if you're on a budget, this museum is free. If you just want to see the building, head here and continue a couple of blocks to the right to a museum that's way more worth it: Museo Jumex; keep reading! ☞

🎟 **Budget:** Free

⊙ **Open:** Daily 10:30am - 6:30pm

♥ **Where:** Plaza Carso (technically not in Polanco, but people always refer to it as Polanco)

🚇 **Address:** Blvrd. Miguel Cervantes Saavedra

@elmuseosoumaya

MUSEO JUMEX

Almost right next to Museo Soumaya you'll find Museo Jumex. Quite the opposite, a subtle, understated building that blends in and harmonizes with its environment. Museo Jumex, in my opinion, has some of the best art the city has to offer. From artworks by Andy Warhol to Cy Twombly, and cool temporary exhibits by the likes of James Turrell. If you're going to hit a museum in Polanco, this is the one.

And bonus...There's an Eno (a cool Mexican breakfast/brunch eatery that you can also find at La Roma) on the ground floor, so you can have some coffee and a bite (try the cookies!) after touring the museum.

Ps. English tours should be booked in advance. Go here to book your tour: ⊕ fundacionjumex.org/en/visita/visitas-guiadas

⚑ **Budget:** Free (but sometimes temporary exhibits have a cost)
⊙ **Open:** Tue - Fri 10am - 5pm / Sat 10am - 7pm / Sun 10am - 5pm - Closed on Mondays
♥ **Where:** Same as Museo Soumaya, technically not in Polanco, but still in Polanco for all intents and purposes of this book
🏛 **Address:** Blvrd. Miguel Cervantes Saavedra 303
@museojumex

BONUS!
ARTE COLECTIVO

Painting while wining and dining? Sign me up! Arte Colectivo was founded by Camila and Martina, two friends with a shared love for art. Now they hold group painting sessions all across the city in cool locations like sushi bars and trendy roof top bars. You don't have to be a painter to join, all you need is openess to meet new friends and to let your creativity out for the night!

⚑ **Budget:** From $25 USD ($500 MXN)
♥ **Where:** The location changes each session!

Shopping in Polanco

The top shopping in Polanco is window shopping along Ave. Masaryk where you find designer stores dripping in high price tags. But hey, it's always fun to look around.

Other than that, here's what we've got…

ANTARA FASHION HALL

The bougiest of them malls, this open plaza should be your destination for some prime shopping. You can find upscale brands like Marc Jacobs, and other more accessible ones like Zara and Sephora. I came here to layer up when I realized my clothes from Puerto Vallarta's beach weather weren't going to suffice for Mexico City spring. I quite enjoyed my afternoon wandering this LA-style open mall. Pro tip! If you happen to be around at Christmas, their decorations are always stunning. One year they even had fake snow falling all around.

○ **Open:** Daily 11am - 8pm
♀ **Where:** Polanco
🛒 **Address:** Ave. Ejército Nacional 843-B
@antara_mx

LAGO DF

Stunning Latin American design pieces. They showcase creators and brands that create decor objects, fashion garments, jewelry, and even art. The prices tend to be steep, but everything they sell is high-end, high quality, and highly unique.

○ **Open:** Daily 11am - 8pm
♀ **Where:** Polanco
🛒 **Address:** Av. Masaryk 310
@lagolatam

Coyoacan & San Angel

•————————•

THE VIBE:

Mexican Small town, colorful and joyful

BEST FOR:

Culture, markets, churros and Frida Kahlo's museum

DAYS NEEDED:

1 or 2 days

•————————•

Coyoacan & San Angel

Coyoacan is in a way the oldest neighborhood in what we today know as Mexico City. It is where the first Spanish settlement was based, where the first colonial palace was built, and where Hernán Cortés directed the construction of the new capital of the Americas. Afterward, the area remained an independent village until it was eventually swallowed by the quickly-developing city in the 20th Century.

Today, it keeps its small-town feel. Cobblestone streets and colorful houses, cheerful plazas alive with families, kids playing and elders catching up. It's an area full of art and joy and things to do and see. Your trip to Mexico City won't be complete without at least a short visit to Coyoacan. It will feel like taking a whole trip outside of Mexico City..and back in time.

Today, it keeps its small-town feel. Cobblestone streets and colorful houses, cheerful plazas alive with families, kids playing and elders catching up. It's an area full of art and joy and things to do and see. Your trip to Mexico City won't be complete without at least a short visit to Coyoacan. It will feel like taking a whole trip outside of Mexico City..and back in time.

And since you're already in the south, you might take a trip a little further down (a 10 min. ride) and visit San Angel. Another little small Mexican postcard of a town engulfed by the concrete jungle. San Angel would seem like a prime tourist spot, but it's still a bit of an off-the-beaten-path area.

Where to Eat in Coyoacan & San Angel

COFFEE & COWORKING

CAFE AVELLANEDA

This place is so tiny that it could be easily overlooked, but thank god you have this book to steer you in the direction of what is arguably the best coffee in Coyoacan. The coffee is amazing, but what I also love about Cafe Avellaneda is that the staff don't treat you like just another tourist. Cafe Avellaneda will become part of your morning routine if you stay nearby. This is also a great place to buy some local coffee to take home, and hey, grab a cookie to take on your walk.

⊙ **Open:** Daily 8am - 9pm
♀ **Where:** Coyoacan
🚽 **Address:** Higuera 40-A
@avellanedakf

CAFE NEGRO

A hip coffee joint in the heart of Coyoacan with artisanal Mexican coffee that has become the coffee spot in the area. Big, cool mugs with bold black letters bring an urban touch to the area´s small-town vibes. Café Negro is always full of travelers taking a break, students catching up on their homework, and hustlers on dates with their laptops. With its mix of wide spacious tables, bars with stools, and smaller, more intimate tables, this coffee place is a perfect place for a coffee break, no matter if you're here to work or play.

⊙ **Open:** Daily 8am - 11pm
♀ **Where:** Coyoacan
🚽 **Address:** Centenario 16 Local B
@cafe_negro_coy

FUN FACT! Coyoacan means "place of coyotes," and that's why there's a fountain with two coyotes in the central plaza.

RUTA DE LA SEDA

This "ecopatisserie", as they call themselves, was the first organic bakery in the city. And in a city that's so crazy about organic and natural stuff, these guys were true pioneers. Café Ruta de la Seda is inspired by the orient, and they have a wide variety of teas besides coffee - and the best matcha latte ever - as well as beautiful, healthy pastries made with organic, sustainable, and fair trade ingredients.

⊙ **Open:** Daily 8am - 10pm
♀ **Where:** Coyoacan
🛱 **Address:** Aurora 1
@rutadelasedamx

BREAKFAST & BRUNCH

SAN ANGEL INN

This is one of Emy's dad's musts for Mexico City, and it's such a classic with tables covered in white linens, servers in formal attire and a Mexican trio (a group of three musicians) playing traditional songs. Either for brunch or lunch, the menu is all Mexican dishes with a trace of international inspiration.

Located inside a former hacienda--turned-monastery with a majestic, beautiful inner courtyard, San Angel Inn is quite the postcard. So much so that, fun fact, Walt Disney World created a tiny duplicate of this place in the Mexico pavilion of their Epcot park.

⊙ **Open:** Breakfast 8am - 11am
Lunch 12pm - 6pm
♀ **Where:** San Angel
🛱 **Address:** Diego Rivera 50

EL OLVIDADO

A quaint and quirky cafe with incredible breakfast inspired by the English countryside and the owner's grandma's cookbook. How cool is that? Besides delicious, organic coffee, they have a wide variety of teas! And lots of English delicacies like scones and a spiced cake along with other European-inspired pastries like Berliners but filled with local fruits like tangerines and mamey.

⊙ **Open:** Mon - Wed 9am - 10pm / Thu 9am - 9pm / Fri - Sun 9am - 10pm
♀ **Where:** Coyoacan
🛱 **Address:** Presidente Venustiano Carranza 267
@elolvidado__

LA MANO

La Mano is a cultural center and artsy garden inspired by and dedicated to art, design and the sweet simplicity of presence. This space is very multi-faceted, holding a coffee shop/eatery, a vintage shop and a venue for events all in one. To be honest, this place has such good coffee that I was going to put it in the coffee section at first, but their menu is equally fresh and comforting and perfect for a brunch moment. The menu is short but with range, featuring dishes like aguachile and a Vietnamese bao with Mexican touches. Check their insta to see their upcoming events, which are as diverse as their menu, going from Biology talks to Oracle Card Readings.

⊙ **Open:** Tue-Sun 9:30am - 8pm

♥ **Where:** A 20 min. Walk from Jardin Hidalgo (the main square)

🚪 **Address:** Francisco Sosa #363

@lamano_jardin

STREET FOOD & LOCAL SPOTS

TOSTADAS COYOACAN (IN THE COYOACAN MARKET)

Head into the market and go straight to find Tostadas Coyoacan (look for the bright yellow sign with red letters). Emy and I ate here by accident without knowing how iconic it was. We were starving, and this place looked good, so we sat, ordered, and were blown away. Tostadas are not something you'll find too often in Mexican cuisine unless you're on the coast. Tostadas are crispy tortillas topped with different ingredients, most commonly ceviche. But here, you'll also find chicken and mole and beef and every Mexican ingredient you can imagine. They're a great snack to have while exploring the market without filling too full like you do with tacos.

⊙ **Open:** Daily 11am - 6pm

♥ **Where:** Inside the Coyoacan Market

🚪 **Address:** Ignacio Allende S/N

LA COCINA DE MI MAMÁ COYOACAN

Another must-try spot in Mercado Coyoacan and a good spot to fill up before heading to the Frida

Kahlo Museum or after. When you order an entree, it usually comes with fresh fruit from the market and a freshwater of the day (agua fresca). Honestly, I'm finding it hard to suggest what to order here because this is the kind of place you could come for breakfast, lunch, and dinner and never have a boring bite. Order something light like ceviche and guacamole, or go all out with some of the best chilaquiles in Mexico City.

La Cocina de mi Mamá Coyoacan is also known for its Mexican craft beer, which pairs perfectly with Chile en Nogada or its ribeye plate served with tortillas and salsas. Whatever you get in this market is going to be made with high-quality ingredients and cooked like your Mexican momma made it. Plus, it's affordable.

Ps. It can be hard to find many things in this maze of a market, so if you're lost, just ask someone Donde está La Cocina de mi Mamá Coyoacan, and they'll point you in the right direction.

⊙ **Open:** Daily 11am - 6pm
♀ **Where:** Inside the Coyoacan Market
🏠 **Address:** Ignacio Allende S/N

LUNCH & DINNER

CORAZÓN DE MAGUEY

Corazón de Maguey is Mexico personified with bright, bold colored walls, crazy art, and piñatas hanging from the ceiling (in a way that doesn't feel like Cinco de Mayo, though!). They define themselves as the "Mezcal's Cathedral," a place to adore and celebrate this Mexican spirit and immerse yourself in the culture around it. Their Mezcal menu focuses mostly on artisanal labels, oh la la.

And to fend off hunger, while you drink, they have many "botanas" (finger food) like quesadillas and even some ceviche. During May-June, they have a "Bug Season," where they offer special dishes that showcase Mexico's favorite insect snacks, such as grasshoppers and ants.

⊙ **Open:** Mon 12:30pm - 11pm / Tue - Thru 8am - 11pm / Fri - Sat 8am - 12am / Sun 8am - 11pm
♀ **Where:** Coyoacan
🏠 **Address:** Jardín Centenario 9A

@corazondemaguey

SWEETS & DESSERTS

LOS DANZANTES

After you've snacked all day at the markets, you might not have room for dinner…but you still might be in the mood to get a little dressed up and have some dessert and cocktails. And honey, this is the place to do it! Los Danzantes is the bougie Instagram food spot of your dreams, especially when it comes to desserts. The main menu always has mixed reviews, but the desserts are consistently fabulous! Come and sit at the bar and try Los Danzantes own brand of Mezcal and order something sweet.

Ps. This place isn't cheap. Think US prices.

Pss. You may or may not need a reservation for sitting at the bar or coming solo, depending on the night. Give them a call beforehand or message them on Instagram to check.

⊙ **Open:** Mon - Thu 12:30pm - 11pm / Fri - Sat 9am - 12pm / Sun 9am - 11pm
♥ **Where:** Coyoacan
🏠 **Address:** Jardín Centenario 12
@losdanzantes
Book at: 55 4356 7185

CHURRERÍA GENERAL DE LA REPÚBLICA

You can't go to Coyoacan without eating some churros…and even better: stuffed churros. This churrería has been around for years and is a local favorite. Their churros are out of this world, sweet and perfectly crispy. You can have your churro with different fillings: the traditional cajeta (a burnt-milk caramel-like sauce that I recommend the most), chocolate, or with fruit-flavored syrup. Pro Tip! Order a hot chocolate and dip your churros.

⊙ **Open:** Daily 9am - 10pm
♥ **Where:** Coyoacan (and a second location inside the Cineteca Nacional)
🏠 **Address:** Allende 38

Drinking Day & Night in Coyoacan & San Angel

LA BIPO

Restaurant by day, modern-day canteen by night. This place is truly bipolar. Not only does it transform when the sun goes down, but the music is also different every day. One night you'll be dancing to some hip hop and rock and roll, while the next, they play electronic music. The ground floor is a chill space, but upstairs is where the party is at. Food-wise, they have a daily menu that mimics homemade food from a Mexican household. Booze-wise, they run daily promos and a permanent promo of a beer and mezcal for $85 pesos. Bottoms up! But drink wisely, always.

⊙ **Open:** Sun -Tue 1pm - 11pm / Wed 1pm - 12am / Thu - Sat 1pm - 2am
♥ **Where:** On the side of Allende Park
🏠 **Address:** Malintzin 155
@LaBipoCoyoacan

LA CELESTINA

The place to go if you want to go out at night in Coyoacan…or if you want to get your day drinking on. You can sit on the sidewalk but try to sit at the bar in their "bunker" area, where the lights dim out for a cozier environment. Try one of their house cocktails or some mezcal with orange slices. And so you don't drink on an empty stomach, they have a small menu full of snacks, both traditional, like shrimp tacos and cactus soup.

⊙ **Open:** Daily 1am - 2pm
♥ **Where:** Coyoacan, right behind the Cathedral
🏠 **Address:** Caballo Calco 14A
@celestina_coyo

PRO TIP! Don't drink mezcal like a shot. Mezcal is to be sipped slowly and by "besitos", little kisses.

Things to Do & See in Coyoacan & San Angel

VISIT FRIDA KAHLO'S HOUSE, AKA LA CASA AZUL

The Frida Kahlo Museum is entirely dedicated to surrealist painter Frida Kahlo. This was her home. This is where she was born, where she lived with her husband, muralist Diego Rivera, and where she died. This museum is also known as La Casa Azul, as it was the name of the house, clearly because of its vibrant cobalt blue walls. This space holds artwork by the artist, but you can also wander around her studio and see some of her personal objects and garments, as well as old photographs of Frida, her family, and her colleagues. Even the bright yellow-tiled kitchen is left as it was, and it's a beautiful insight into life in Mexico in the early 1990s.

This museum alone put Coyoacan on the map for visitors. While it has become a landmark for visitors in the past few years, just ten years ago, it was still not even that known. Even most of Emy's Mexican friends had never even been. But today, there are lines around the corner to go in, and tickets are sold out days (if not weeks) in advance. I recommend buying your tickets online, so you don't miss out ⊕museofridakahlo.org.mx

🔖 **Budget:** $250 pesos on weekdays / $270 pesos on weekends + $30 pesos fee to take photos inside
⊙ **Open:** Tue 10am - 6pm / Wed 11am - 6pm / Thu - Sun 10am - 6pm
📍 **Where:** Coyoacan
🏛 **Address:** Londres 247
@museofridakahlo

Want to skip the lines? Go on this bike tour which includes a visit to Frida's, literally called "Frida VIP-skip the Line + Bikes & Churros"

PORTRAIT OF FRIDA, BY HER FATHER, GUILLERMO KAHLO

A NOTE ABOUT FRIDA KAHLO...

Frida has become some kind of post-mortem spokesperson for Mexican tourism. You'll see her in every possible souvenir available, in every shop, on every corner. I've even seen embroidered Frida bags in traditional markets in Bali. That's how widespread her image has become. If you're going to buy a souvenir with her face plastered on it, I think it's best to learn at least a little bit of the story behind this formidable woman. So here's a super short crash course on Frida Kahlo and why she became the female icon she is…

Madgalena Frieda Kahlo y Calderón, aka Frida Kahlo, was born in 1907 in Coyoacan. Her father was German, and her mother was Mexican of Native American descent. She had a tumultuous childhood, suffering from polio from an early age. As a teenager, she was involved in a bus accident that left her with severe injuries for which she had to undergo over 30 surgeries throughout her life. She is best known for her bright and colorful paintings, most of them self-portraits that deal with themes such as her identity, the contrast between life and death, and pain. You can see many elements related to her medical issues throughout her work, like the corset-like casts she constantly had to wear.

She first became known as Diego Rivera's wife, but her own work became notorious in the 1930s, and her first solo exhibition was held in New York. One of her pieces was the first painting by a Mexican artist of the 20th Century to be acquired by the Louvre Museum. In short, she was one of the first female painters in Mexico who was recognized and celebrated for her work.

Why am I telling all of this? Because a woman shouldn't be just revered by her image. Frida Kahlo isn't an icon because of her colorful representation of Mexican culture. She is an icon because she was bold, brave, and resilient, and there's so much more to her than being the designated Mexican postcard. So here, you can now bring a Frida souvenir back home but also tell the tale of badassness behind her uni-brow and floral headdresses.

PRO TIP! If you want to learn more, the movie "Frida" (yep, the one with Salma Hayek) is a pretty good and authentic depiction of her life. Watch it before your trip so you can enjoy her museum even more.

MUSICAL FUN FACT! Coldplay's album "Viva La Vida" is named after a painting by Frida Kahlo. The band visited La Casa Azul (Frida's Museum) in 2007 and decided to pay homage to her joyful approach to life despite her ailments and perpetual state of physical pain.

MERCADO DE COYOACAN

A traditional and iconic market full of life and color all around you! Narrow alleyways packed with vegetables, colorful piñatas, and the most random knick-knacks. You'll see tourists here buying souvenirs, but this is a local market with mostly local clientele buying their groceries and eating at the many food stalls. How is this market different from others you can find in the city? It comes with a tad more authenticity as Coyoacan isn't as gentrified as other trendy neighborhoods.

⊙ **Open:** Daily 8am - 8pm
♥ **Where:** Coyoacan
🛒 **Address:** Ignacio Allende S/N

MUSEO ANAHUACALLI

Frida Kahlo has La Casa Azul, and Diego Rivera has the Anahuacalli museum. In this temple-like house, you can explore some of Diego's murals and his personal collection of over 1500 pre-hispanic pieces. This place is not only a testament to Diego's legacy but to ancestral Mexico as well. While this place is not exactly in the heart of Coyoacan, it is just a short ride away from it. Note: You're not allowed to record videos in the museum.

🖌 **Budget:** $100 pesos for foreigners / $80 pesos for nationals + $30 pesos fee to take photos
⊙ **Open:** Tue - Sun 11am - 5:30pm
♥ **Where:** Coyoacan
🛫 **Address:** Museo 150
⊕ https://museoanahuacalli.org.mx/en/#museo

MUSEO CASA ESTUDIO DIEGO RIVERA Y FRIDA KAHLO

So far we have Frida Kahlo's house as a museum, and Diego Rivera's house as a museum. But there's a third one: a house in San Angel where they lived together on and off for 20 years. This house was designed and built specifically for them: two separate buildings united by a bridge. Each artist had their own space, but their worlds were still united. Inside you'll find small exhibits for both Frida and Diego and Diego's painting studio. But beyond what lies inside, this house is mostly known for its architecture, with bright red floor-to-ceiling window panels, cobalt blue walls, and its iconic cacti fence. Come here if you've been in Mexico City for a while and already visited both museums above, or if you want a glimpse into these artists' lives while avoiding the crowds.

🖌 **Budget:** $40 pesos
⊙ **Open:** Tue - Sun 11am - 5pm
♥ **Where:** San Angel
🛫 **Address:** Ave. Altavista corner with Diego Rivera

RIDE THE COYOACAN TRAM

The area to explore in Coyoacan is fairly small, and you can do it on foot. But there's an even more fun way: aboard a classic old-style tram. These bright-red carriages are restored original trams that used to run across Coyoacan when it was just a town on the outskirts of Mexico City. Their daytime tours explore all the points of interest around Coyoacan, like La Casa Azul, but at night time, they switch to a Myths and Legends Tour, and they even have a "canteen to canteen" tour.

💸 **Budget:** $80 pesos
◎ **Open:** Daily 10am - 6pm
📍 **Where:** The tour begins at Jardin Hidalgo
🏠 **Address:** Jardin Plaza Hidalgo S/N

MUAC

A contemporary museum right on the campus of the National Autonomous University of Mexico. It holds avant-garde and often disruptive, temporary exhibits and a permanent collection of works of art from 1952 onward. This museum attracts contemporary art aficionados and architecture lovers alike because of the leading-edge building that holds the museum.

💸 **Budget:** $40 pesos
◎ **Open:** Wed - Sun 11am - 6pm
📍 **Where:** inside UNAM - National Autonomous University of Mexico
🏠 **Address:** Insurgentes Sur 3000

BOLERAMA COYOACAN

Not the most Mexican thing to do, but if you've been around for a while, this is such a fun thing to do with your new travel friends. Or a great plan for a date to break the cup of coffee/glass of wine routine! Bolerama Coyoacan was one of the first bowling alleys in the country and it keeps its retro vibes, Big Lebowski style. The snacks are great, and you can drink some beer or a cocktail while you play. Ps. There's a flamingo somewhere in this place's walls. Can you spot it? Take a photo and tag me! ⊕ @sologirlstravelguide

💸 **Budget:** Mon - Thu $450 / Fri - Sat $550 / Sun $399

*prices are per hour and per track + $35 shoe rental fee

⊘ **Open:** Mon - Wed 1pm - 10pm / Thu - Fri 1pm - 12am / Sat 12pm - 12am / Sun 12pm - 10pm

📍 **Where:** Coyoacan

🏠 **Address:** Eje Sur 8

CINETECA NACIONAL

The Cineteca Nacional is the National Film Archives, and it first opened in 1974. Since then, it's been dedicated to the preservation of film in Mexico, and gathers thousands of cinephiles for screenings every month. Their film roster consists mostly of art films and documentaries, but they also show movies with less-common topics like sexual diversity and even some artsy erotica films.

Besides their projection room, they also hold screenings in their open air forum, where you can lay on the grass and have a picnic with your movie. The building alone is remarkable and worth the visit.

💸 **Budget:**

Cinema $60 pesos / $40 pesos for visitors under 25 years old

Open Air Forum Tue - Thu Free / Fri - Sun $70 pesos

⊘ **Open:** From 1:30 pm on weekdays / 11am on weekends

📍 **Where:** Coyoacan

🏠 **Address:** Ave. Mexico-Coyoacan 389

Shopping in Coyoacan & San Angel

BAZAR DEL SÁBADO

Back in the 1960s, a group of artisans decided to unite and create their own space where they could showcase their work. That is how Bazar del Sabado was born. The name translates as Saturday's Bazar, a bazaar that happens every Saturday where you can find every kind of Mexican craft possible. It's a whole trip around the arts & crafts world in just one morning. Bazar del Sábado is held inside a gorgeous old house with a small plaza outside that fills with local artists selling their artworks. You can wander both inside the home and in the plaza.

PRO TIP! Come early because it's gonna get crowded as the day progresses.

⊙ **Open:** Saturdays 10am - 7pm
♀ **Where:** San Angel
🏛 **Address:** Plaza San Jacinto 11
@bazaarsabado

MERCADO ARTESANAL MEXICANO

Another traditional market in Coyoacan, except this one, is entirely dedicated to arts and crafts. Inside you'll find ceramic, woven crafts, traditional toys, and anything from the colorful world that Mexican crafts are. This market is less touristy and less crowded than La Ciudadela crafts market downtown, so prices will be cheaper and the experience a bit more authentic. Ps. Don't forget it's always alright to haggle just a little bit.

⊙ **Open:** Mon - Thu 11am - 8pm / Fri - Sun 11am 9pm
♀ **Where:** Coyoacan
🏛 **Address:** Felipe Carrillo Puerto 25

THINGS TO KNOW BEFORE
COMING TO
Mexico City

Festivals & Holidays in Mexico

Mexico is a catholic country, so you'll find that many of the holidays and festivities are religion-based while others are historical milestones. But no matter the occasion, Mexicans love any reason to get together and celebrate. And man, do Mexicans know how to celebrate!

Without further adieu, let me introduce you to a few of the most significant holidays in Mexico...

HOLIDAYS

DAY OF THE DEAD - *November 2nd*

Day of the Dead has become one of Mexico's most iconic celebrations, mostly for the stunning skull-like face paint, flower headbands, and opulent jewelry that floods Instagram every year.

📷 GENARO SERVIN

It's believed that on the Day of the Dead, those who have passed away come back to earth to visit. And rather than mourning death, Mexicans celebrate life! Mexicans visit their deceased ones' tombstones or set up tiered altars displaying symbolic gifts like marigold flowers, candles, and food. And at the very top of the altar, family members will display a photo of whomever that altar is dedicated to.

You'll find that in Mexico, death is not something to be afraid of. It is mourned, of course. But death is celebrated with humor, irreverence, and joy. Try it out. See how it feels.

EMY'S SUPER DUPER PRO TIP!

Watch the movie Coco, by Disney Pixar. It's a very accurate and beautiful representation of this holiday and culture from Central Mexico.

CINCO DE MAYO - *May 5th*

Guess what? I'm about to burst your bubble when I tell you that Cinco the Mayo is not a thing in Mexico. Mexicans don't really celebrate it. And no, it's not Mexican Independence Day. But yes, it is a historic holiday that celebrates the victory of the Mexican Army against a French Invasion back in 1862. Cinco de Mayo is actually one of the least celebrated holidays in Mexico. If you find yourself in a Cinco de Mayo celebration...you're in a (very) tourisT spot. Still, Mexicans will never say no to celebration. So, in local fashion, go ahead and down that tequila anyway.

INDEPENDENCE DAY - *September 16th*

That being said...the real Mexican Independence Day is celebrated on the eve of September 15th to ring in the 16th. Kinda like New Year's, but with tequila instead of champagne. Lots and lots of tequila. If you're around for this day, you will find parties and celebrations pretty much everywhere. From traditional parties to nightclub events.

CHRISTMAS EVE - *December 24th*

Being such a family-oriented and Catholic culture, Christmas is a big deal in México. The biggest celebration is Christmas Eve (Noche Buena), where people get together, have dinner, and exchange presents. And on the 25th, they get together again and have a leftovers feast. However, with such American influence, Christmas in Puerto Vallarta looks a bit like it does in the US. Expect to behold sparkling lights, Santas, and reindeers all around.

LADY DE GUADALUPE - *December 12th*

The Lady of Guadalupe is Mexico's representation of the Virgin Mary. And they say that even the most atheists in Mexico are "guadalupanos" (devotees of the Lady of Guadalupe). She's the mother of all Mexicans, and she is celebrated in a BIG way. Special masses are held. People pilgrimage for days. Flowers and serenades are delivered to church. And even many businesses are closed.

LABOR DAY – *May 1st*

Not a holiday that's hugely celebrated, but most businesses will be closed on Labor Day. And sometimes, since Cinco de Mayo falls shortly after Labor Day, this weekend will become one big long weekend!

SEMANA SANTA (AKA MEXICAN SPRING BREAK)

Also dependent on the Catholic Church's calendar, the dates of Semana Santa change every year but usually fall in the spring time between March and April. Semana Santa means Holy Week, but it's pretty much the opposite of holy, if you know what I mean. School is out for two weeks, and that means a lot of locals flee the city to go to the beach. Leaving a calmer, less crowded Mexico City for you to enjoy.

FESTIVALS IN MEXICO CITY

CORONA CAPITAL / *November*

Corona Capital is Mexico's Coachella. Three days of concerts with an international line-up. It happens every year in the Fall, and the line-up is released in early summer. The last edition included headliners like Miley Cyrus, Paramore, The 1975, and Arctic Monkeys, among others. Get your tickets at ⊕ coronacapital.com.mx

VIVE LATINO / *March*

Another music festival, but with a focus on Latin American music. Both national and international bands perform in a span of 3 days. Most of the music will be in Spanish, so this is a great cultural-language immersion experience. Although usually there are also some non-Latin performers on the line-up. Get your tickets at ⊕ vivelatino.com.mx

ART WEEK

Art lovers, pay attention. As if Mexico City wasn't artsy enough, the city is also home to Latin America's biggest contemporary art fair. This is a very cool time to come to Mexico City, even if you don't go to the fair. There are satellite parties and events in galleries, restaurants, and bars all around the city. It's held every year in early February. Start by checking out these events:

→ Zona Maco: zonamaco.com

→ Material Art Fair:

→ Zona Acme:

DESIGN WEEK MEXICO (DWM) / *October*

Design Week is a series of events and spaces spread throughout the city in the span of a week. All related mostly to design in all its forms, but also to art and architecture. You can see work by big names in the design world and get to know up-and-comers. And same as with Zona Maco, DWM is a great time to visit the city because of all the events going on around it. Especially in neighborhoods like Roma, Condesa, and Polanco. Visit ⊕ designweekmexico.com for more.

FESTIVAL DEL DÍA DE MUERTOS / *Last days of October - First days of November*

Now that you know all about the Day of the Dead, you can plan your trip to Mexico City to be around to join the festivities. Witness the annual parade that flows down Ave. Reforma and Ave. Juarez to the Zocalo, which is filled with offerings. All along the way, you'll see people dressed up at catrinas, with painted faces and flower headdresses.

Even though the Day of the Dead is on Nov 2nd, the celebrations extend to the days prior. You'll see the city dressed up in colorful "papel picado" (those colorful papercut banners), and marigolds. And beautiful altars are set up all around town. Eat all the pan de muerto, drink all the chocolate caliente and soak it all in. Día de Los Muertos is truly an explosion of color and culture.

LOOKING FOR MORE EVENTS WITH LIKE-MINDED GIRLS WHILE IN MEXICO CITY?

"Chicas Chidas by LEI" is a group of badass girls who hold unique events across the world, fostering female empowerment, leadership, and creativity; as well as a sense of community and togetherness among girls.

Their events are mostly about art and gastronomy and often about the dialogue between the two. They arrange happenings and hybrid events like dinners and art exhibits, or wine tastings where a female DJ provides the soundtrack.

This community was born in Mexico City, but they have chapters in Bali, New York, Paris, London, Madrid, Barcelona, and Singapore. So if you're going to any of those places, check out what they have going on too!

Follow them at @chicaschidasbylei

Frequently Asked Questions

Is Mexico City Safe? Overall, Mexico City is a safe destination, but there are still some recommended precautions to take to avoid petty crime and scams. Take your basic precautions and stay in the neighborhoods mentioned in this guidebook. Read more about safety tips on page 76.

How do I make friends in Mexico City? Traveling solo and want to make friends fast? Just introduce yourself in Girls in Mexico City (use the hashtag #HeyImAwesome) and ask if anyone wants to grab a drink. Also, carry one of the Solo Girls Tote Bags. It's not just a bag, it's also our official signal to other solo female travelers that you're open to meeting new people! Get the bags in my travel store ⊕ Alexa-West.com/travel-shop

Can I bring my dog to Mexico City? Yes, and it's not too complicated. You'll just need to follow a simple process: get your dog's health certificate, fill out the right forms and have your dog inspected by the authorities when you land. Don't forget to check your airline requirements if you're traveling by air.

✳ Want to add more FAQs to the list? Reach out to me and let me know at alexa@alexa-west.com

MINI
Directory
FOR MEXICO CITY

IMPORTANT NUMBERS

Dial 911 in case of an emergency

Local Police - +52 322 178 8999

The Green Angels (Free Roadside Assistance) - 078

Red Cross Emergencies - 065

Red Cross Ambulances - 066

Red Cross - +52 322 222 1533

Locatel (Mexico City's information line) - +52 5556581111

Tourist Assistance Hotline - 8000089090

EMBASSIES

U.S. Embassy
+52 55 5080 2000

Canadian Embassy
+52 55 5724 7900

HOW TO CALL MEXICAN NUMBERS FROM A FOREIGN NUMBER

Let's say you're given this number: 55 5080 2000

If you just type that number in your phone, it might not work.

Solution: drop the 0 and add the country code (+52)

So now the number looks like this:

+52 55 5080 2000

OVER THE COUNTER BIRTH CONTROL

CONDOMS

Easy to get everywhere.

PILLS

You can buy birth control pills and contraception over the counter in Mexico at pharmacies.

Where: All pharmacies, but the two recommended ones are Ahorro Pharmacy and Guadalajara Farmacia.

Pills to Ask for: Levonorgestrel

Depo Shot to Ask for: Cyclofemina 200 pesos at Farmacia Ahorro, they give you the needle, and you can inject yourself at home…not kidding.

MORNING AFTER PILL

Where: Most pharmacies carry it under the name Femelle One, Post Day, or Levonelle

Please make sure you've come to Mexico with Travel Insurance.

If you don't have it yet, go to
Alexa-West.com or scan this code ☞

THE TRUE STORY OF HOW THE
Solo Girl's Travel Guide
WAS BORN

I was robbed in Cambodia.

Sure, the robber was a child and yes, I might have drunkenly put my purse down in the sand while flirting with an irresistible Swedish boy… but that doesn't change the fact that I found myself without cash, a debit card and hotel key at 1am in a foreign country.

My mini robbery, however, doesn't even begin to compare to my other travel misadventures. I've also been scammed to tears by taxi drivers, idiotically taken ecstasy in a country with the death penalty for drugs and missed my flight because how was I supposed to know that there are two international airports in Bangkok?

It's not that I'm a total idiot.
It's just that…people aren't born savvy travelers.

I'm not talking about hedonistic vacationers who spend their weekend at a resort sipping Mai Tais. I'm talking about train-taking, market-shopping, street food-eating travelers!

Traveling is not second (or third or fourth) nature; it's a skill that only comes with sweaty on-the-ground experience…especially for women!

In the beginning of my travels (aka the first 5 years), I made oodles of travel mistakes. And thank god I did. These mistakes eventually turned me into the resourceful, respected and established travel guru that I am today.

Year-after-year and country-after-country, I started learning things like...

✔Always check your hostel mattress for bed bugs.

✔ Local alcohol is usually toxic and will give you a hangover that lasts for days.

✔ The world isn't "touristy" once you stop traveling like a tourist.

✔ And most importantly, the best noodle shops are always hidden in back alleys.

After nearly 11 years of traveling solo around the world (4 continents and 26 countries, but who's counting?) – I travel like a gosh darn pro. I save money, sleep better, haggle harder, fly fancier, and speak foreign languages that help me almost almost blend in with the locals despite my blonde hair.

Yeah yeah yeah. I guess it's cool being a travel icon. But shoot...

Do you know how much money, how many panic attacks, and how many life-threatening risks I could have saved and/or avoided if only someone had freakin' queued me into all of this precious information along the way? A lot. A lotta' lot.

So, why didn't I just pick up a travel guide and start educating myself like an adult? I had options...right? I could've bought a copy of Lonely Planet...but how the hell am I supposed to smuggle a 5-pound brick in my carry-on bag? Or DK Eyewitness, perhaps? Hell no. I don't have 8 hours to sift through an encyclopedia and decode details relevant to my solo adventure.

There was no travel guide that would have spared my tears or showed me how to travel safer and smarter.

The book I needed didn't exist. So, I freakin' wrote it myself.

What travel guide do you need me to write next?

Tell me on Instagram ♥ @sologirlstravelguide

THE 11 TRAVEL COMMANDMENTS
of the Solo Girl's Travel Guide

01 — BE AN EXPLORER, NOT A TOURIST.

Some people travel just for the photo. While others travel to find the unfamiliar, connect with strangers, expand their minds, and try new things for the sake of trying new things. Which kind of traveler are you?

02 — LEAVE ROOM FOR HAPPENSTANCE

Don't overstuff your itinerary. Slow down, be where you are and leave room for serendipity! Literally, schedule serendipity time so the universe can take the lead.

03 — VOTE WITH YOUR DOLLAR

When possible, choose to support local businesses that operate ethically - aka businesses that respect the environment, benefit their local communities, don't take advantage of animals and just treat their staff really really well.

04 — LOOK FOR THE GIFT

Love your mistakes! With every bump in the road comes a gift. Miss a bus? Look for the gift. Lose your room key? Look for the gift. Get dumped on your honeymoon? Look for the gift! There will always be a gift.

05 — STAY CURIOUS

Ask questions! Ask questions when you like something and ask questions when you don't understand something. Out loud or in your head. And whenever you feel judgment arise, replace it with a question instead.

06 — MORE STORIES, LESS PHOTOS

Take a couple photos and then put your phone away. While everyone else is taking shitty sunset photos that never look as good on camera... you are really there, experiencing every shade of color in real time. Take note in your head of the story you will bring home - of the people you see, the food you smell, the monkeys in the trees! Look up, not down.

07 — COUNT EXPERIENCES, NOT PASSPORT STAMPS

You can never "do" Mexico. You can go to Mexico 50 times and still each experience will be different than the last. Travel to live, not to brag.

08 — MIND YOUR IMPACT

Leave every place better than you found it. Take a piece of trash from the beach and be kind to people you meet. Bring your own water bottle, canvas bag, and reusable straw to avoid single-use plastics.

09 — AVOID VOLUNTOURISM

People are not zoo animals. Playing with children at orphanages, temporarily teaching English in villages or volunteering at women's shelters hurt more than they help. Want to volunteer with a positive impact? Check out my blog at Alexa-West.com

10 — CARRY YOUR POSITIVITY

Ever had a crappy day and then a stranger smiles at you and flips your entire mood? Travel can be hard, but your positivity will be your secret weapon. Happy vibes are contagious. Even when we don't speak the local language, a smile or a random act of kindness tips the universal scale in the right direction for you and the people you meet along your journey.

11 — TRUST YOUR GUT

Listen to that little voice inside you. When something doesn't feel right, back away. When something feels good, lean. Your intuition will lead you to beautiful places, unforgettable moments, and new lifelong friends.

BONUS: Drink where the Locals Drink, Eat Where the Locals Eat

Even if it's under a tarp outside a mini mart. This is how you discover the best food and make the most meaningful connections.

It feeeeeeeels good to travel good.

A CONFESSION:

I bend the rules. Sometimes I stay in an all-inclusive resort instead of a locally owned guesthouse. Sometimes I go to McDonald's because I want a taste of home. And sometimes, especially when I'm tired or hungry, I'm not all sunshine and rainbows to be around.

But my moral travel compass does not bend for things that matter to me. I'll never leave a piece of trash on the beach. I'll never support elephant riding. I'd rather stay home than go on a Carnival Cruise even if it was free. Decide what matters to you now, let that guide you as you travel but let yourself be human.

Comfort yourself when you need comforting and eat the forbidden fruit sparingly. When you do make mistakes, brush yourself off and do better next time. No one's path is perfect but I'm proud of you for making your path better.

THIS TRIP.

THIS IS WHEN YOU DISCOVER EXACTLY WHO YOU ARE.

TRUST YOURSELF.

DO YOU HAVE
THIS BOOK YET?

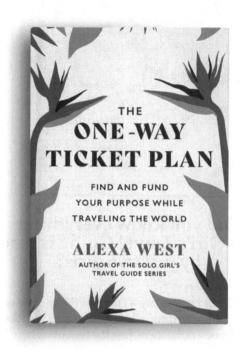

THE ONE-WAY TICKET PLAN

FIND AND FUND YOUR PURPOSE
WHILE TRAVELING THE WORLD

••••••••••••

GET IT AT ALEXA-WEST.COM

••••••••••••

Did you know everything Solo Girl's Travel Guide is made by just two girls?

That's right, just me and my #TravelBFF Emy. We do all the research, traveling, writing, editing, fact checking, designing... No fancy publishers, just the two of us here.

Want to buy us a coffee while we work on bringing you the next book? We'll pass it on by supporting local businesses around the world.

Buy us a coffee at buymeacoffee.com/sgtg

You an also follow our adventures on Insta as we create more books for you.

@sologirlstravelguide | @__helloemilia

DID YOU LEAVE A REVIEW?

As a self-published author –
doing this whole publishing thing by myself
–

reviews are what keeps
The Solo Girl's Travel Guide growing.

If you found my guidebook to be helpful,
please leave me a review on <u>Amazon.com</u>

Your review helps other girls find this book
and experience a truly life-changing trip.

Ps. I read every single review.

WHERE NEXT?

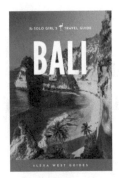

BALI

THAILAND

VIETNAM

SOUTH KOREA

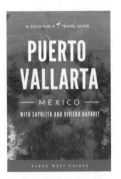

PUERTO VALLARTA & RIVIERA NAYARIT

CAMBODIA

And More...
Get The Whole Collection.

Made in United States
Troutdale, OR
05/04/2024

19645383R00156